Writing to Change the World

ALSO BY MARY PIPHER

Letters to a Young Therapist (2003)

The Middle of Everywhere:
Helping Refugees Enter the American Community (2002)

Another Country: Navigating the Emotional Terrain of Our Elders (2000)

Hunger Pains: The Modern Woman's Tragic Quest for Thinness (1997)

The Shelter of Each Other: Rebuilding Our Families (1996)

Reviving Ophelia: Saving the Selves of Adolescent Girls (1994)

Writing to Change the World

MARY PIPHER

RIVERHEAD BOOKS
a member of
PENGUIN GROUP (USA) INC.
NEW YORK
2006

RIVERHEAD BOOKS
Published by the Penguin Group
Penguin Group (USA) Inc., 375 Hudson Street, New York, New York 10014, USA • Penguin Group (Canada),
90 Eglinton Avenue East, Suite 700, Toronto, Ontario M4P 2Y3, Canada (a division of Pearson Penguin
Canada Inc.) • Penguin Books Ltd, 80 Strand, London WC2R 0RL, England • Penguin Ireland, 25 St Stephen's
Green, Dublin 2, Ireland (a division of Penguin Books Ltd) • Penguin Group (Australia), 250 Camberwell Road,
Camberwell, Victoria 3124, Australia (a division of Pearson Australia Group Pty Ltd) • Penguin Books India Pvt
Ltd, 11 Community Centre, Panchsheel Park, New Delhi–110 017, India • Penguin Group (NZ), Cnr Airborne and
Rosedale Roads, Albany, Auckland 1310, New Zealand (a division of Pearson New Zealand Ltd) • Penguin Books
(South Africa) (Pty) Ltd, 24 Sturdee Avenue, Rosebank, Johannesburg 2196, South Africa

Penguin Books Ltd, Registered Offices:
80 Strand, London WC2R 0RL, England

Library of Congress Cataloging-in-Publication Data

Pipher, Mary Bray.
Writing to change the world / Mary Pipher.
p. cm.
Includes bibliographical references.
ISBN 1-59448-920-3
1. Authorship—Social aspects. 2. Authorship—Psychological aspects. 3. Literature and society. I. Title.
PN145.P486 2006 2005055085
808'.02—dc22

Printed in the United States of America
1 3 5 7 9 10 8 6 4 2

Book design by Stephanie Huntwork

While the author has made every effort to provide accurate telephone numbers and Internet addresses at the time
of publication, neither the publisher nor the author assumes any responsibility for errors, or for changes that occur
after publication. Further, the publisher does not have any control over and does not assume any responsibility for
author or third-party websites or their content.

To Anne Frank and Nelson Mandela and to those

writers from all over the world who, in all times

and places, have written to make things better

You write in order to change the world, knowing perfectly well that you probably can't, but also knowing that literature is indispensable to the world. . . . The world changes according to the way people see it, and if you alter, even by a millimeter, the way . . . people look at reality, then you can change it.

—JAMES BALDWIN

Contents

Calls to Action

Writing to Change the World

INTRODUCTION

> More than at any time in history mankind faces a cross-roads. One path leads to despair and utter hopelessness, the other to total extinction. Let us pray that we will have the wisdom to choose correctly. —WOODY ALLEN

Maybe things are not quite as bad as Woody Allen suggests, but they are bad enough. Life has never been easy, but today the scope of problems that befall us is greater than ever before. Up until this last hundred years, humans were expected to deal only with their immediate environment. If they were hungry, they planted grain, went fishing, or foraged. If their children cried or their parents lay dying, they could caress them and sing to them. When it was cold, they built fires. When an animal or another human attacked, they tried to fend it or him off. The problems that arose often were not solvable. But they were nearby.

For the most part, humans had little idea what was happening over the next mountain, let alone continents away. They knew only what they could see, smell, hear, taste, and touch. If they spotted ripe blueberries, they could pick them for dinner. And adults knew what they could do for one another. If a neighbor's hut burned down, they could help build another. If children were left without parents, they could take them in.

Today our senses are amplified by technology. We receive detailed information from all over the globe. Daily, we see buildings collapsing, children starving, and whole villages dying of AIDS. Our brains and our adrenal systems have electrical and chemical responses to world events, yet our bodies, which are far from these troubles, can do little to help. Many of us become anxious and despair from this poisonous brew of overstimulation and powerlessness.

I can name salient examples of our harsh world—the deterioration of the ozone layer, deforestation, and the enormous differences in wealth across nations and within our own. We live in a world where twenty-seven million people live in slavery, a world where poor children make toys for rich children, where the World Food Program cuts distribution because of lack of funds while two-thirds of Americans fight obesity. We humans have become the species of nuclear weapons and genocide, one that is killing itself and all other living things.

Right now, our beautiful democracy is eroding before our eyes, as, for example, our government disregards the Geneva Conventions and uses torture as a method of interrogation; in the history of our country, this has never been official policy. As has often been the case historically, power is distributed according to wealth, not wisdom or compassion. Bullies and thugs rule the world. Increasingly, it feels as if we are trapped in a medieval crisis—Crusaders versus Jihadists. The Enlightenment is in remission, and science is simultaneously exploited and ignored. Technology advances rapidly as collective wisdom declines. We are a nation good at consuming and poor at savoring. In my thirty years of being a therapist, I have never seen

Americans more stressed. If the news were a weather report, every day it would be the same: Black clouds overhead. Tornado warning!

> I feel the vacuum, the loneliness, the silence, the dehydration of the soul as people who want desperately to save our constitution, country and planet still wander the streets without knowing how to say hi to one another.   —SAM SMITH
>
> Distance negates responsibility.   —GUY DAVENPORT

We live together in an era of what Anthony Lewis, a columnist for *The New York Times,* has called "existential blindness." *Tech Tonic,* a publication of the Alliance for Childhood, reports that the average American can recognize over a thousand brand names but is unable to identify ten indigenous plants or animals. We understand many facts about the world, but we cannot discern their meaning or their implications for action. Our world needs leaders, and yet people everywhere feel helpless and lack direction.

While we call our time the Age of Information, wisdom is in short supply. Language, which maps the ways we think, is often just another marketing tool. Style trumps substance. War is called peace, while destruction is called development. Environmental devastation is footnoted or ignored. Hype and spin trivialize and obscure the truth. My favorite example of fuzzy language is George Tenet's line during congressional hearings in spring 2004. When questioned on inaccurate government information regarding weapons of mass destruction, he said, "The data do not uniquely comport with policy decisions." Parse that.

Sometimes language itself is a weapon. In urging a crackdown on asylum seekers, people who have fled their countries without valid documents, James Sensenbrenner, a congressman from Wisconsin, said that he wanted to "Stop terrorists from gaming the asylum system." He failed to mention that no asylum seekers have been identified as having links to terrorists. And, clearly, he does not know the asylum seekers I know—Tibetan monks fleeing Chinese soldiers, human rights advocates escaping from repressive governments, some of America's greatest friends who are leaving countries where rulers fear democracy.

Language is weaponized when it is used to objectify, depersonalize, dehumanize, to create an "other." Once a person is labeled as "not like us," the rules for civilized behavior no longer apply. The phrase "illegal alien" is an obvious example. Both the word "illegal" and the word "alien" separate us from the person being described. Indeed, America treats illegal aliens quite badly. The truth is that no person is illegal and no person is alien.

Kay Daly, of the Coalition for a Fair Judiciary, missile-launches language to maim and kill. She is writing about what she calls "the Left": "You know who they are. You've seen them. The pro-abortion fanatics and the radical feminists; the atheists who file lawsuits attacking the Pledge of Allegiance and the Ten Commandments; the environmentalist, tree-hugging animal rights extremists; the one-world globalists who worship at the altar of the United Nations; the militant homosexuals and the anti-military hippie peaceniks. . . ." Daly isn't talking about people or ideas: she is disconnecting and demonizing—processes that have led to disastrous consequences in our last century.

Musician Ted Nugent objectified others when he addressed the NRA: "I want carjackers dead. I want rapists dead. I want burglars

dead. I want child molesters dead. I want the bad guys dead. No
court case. No parole, no early release. I want 'em dead. Get a gun
and when they attack you, shoot 'em."

Progressives also have their ways of dehumanizing. They hurl
stones when they use terms such as "fundamentalists," "rednecks,"
or "right-wing conservatives" in derisive ways that allow no room
for nuances, individual differences, or empathy with their adversaries' points of view.

I am not interested in weapons, whether words or guns. I want to
be part of the rescue team for our tired, overcrowded planet. The
rescuers will be those people who help other people to think clearly,
and to be honest and open-minded. They will be an antidote to those
people who disconnect us. They will de-objectify, rehumanize, and
make others more understandable and sympathetic. They will help
create what philosopher Martin Buber called I-thou relationships for
the human race.

Buber distinguished between "I-it" and "I-thou" relationships. In
I-it relationships, we deal with living creatures in one-dimensional
ways. An "it" exists merely to serve our own purposes. A bank teller
is essentially a nonperson who gives us our money; an old-growth
forest is lumber waiting to be harvested. In an I-thou relationship,
the bank teller is a person like us, with desires, dreams, and people
she loves. And an old-growth forest has a purpose far greater than
our wish for lumber. When we deal with the teller or the forest in
I-thou ways, we show respect. We are entering into a relationship.

Once the concept of otherness takes root, the unimaginable becomes possible. We don't want to look at the faces of the homeless
as we walk past them; when we do, they become people, and it becomes harder to keep walking. During the Vietnam War, our GIs

called the Vietcong "gooks"; in Iraq, our soldiers call the insurgents "rats" and their trails "ratlines." Psychologically, humans can kill rats much more easily then they can kill hungry, tired, frightened young people much like themselves.

With connection comes responsibility. Without it, decent Americans vote for government policies or support businesses that leave villages in India or Africa without drinking water. We do this by erasing from our consciousness any awareness that our actions have hurtful consequences for people whose names we do not know. Labels help. It's easy to erase "civilians," "peasants," "insurgents," "enemy combatants," even "protestors." Once we have a label that doesn't fit us, we can ignore the humanity of the labeled. Part of our responsibility as writers is to tell stories that make such erasures impossible.

A writer's job is to tell stories that connect readers to all the people on earth, to show these people as the complicated human beings they really are, with histories, families, emotions, and legitimate needs. We can replace one-dimensional stereotypes with multidimensional individuals with whom our readers can identify. In creating a world of I-thou relationships, writers can do much of the heavy lifting.

Go to the street corners and invite to the banquet anyone you find.   —MATTHEW 22:10

Everything is hitched to everything else.   —JOHN MUIR

We are one leaf on the great human tree. —PABLO NERUDA

The emergent science of ecology is easily summed up: Everything is connected. But interconnection is anathema to a consumer notion of the world, where each of us is useful precisely to the degree that we consider ourselves the center of everything.   —BILL MCKIBBEN

Writing for Change

Good writing facilitates the making of connections in a way that inspires openheartedness, thinking, talking, and action. All totalitarian governments achieve their ends by frightening and isolating people, and by preventing honest public discussion of important matters. The way to promote social and economic justice is by doing just the opposite: by telling the truth, and by encouraging civil, public discussion.

Good writing enlarges readers' knowledge of the world, or empowers readers to act for the common good, or even inspires other good writing. We all understand the world from our own point of view, our own frames of reference, that allow us to make sense of what our senses take in. Writers help readers construct larger, more expansive frames of reference so that more of the world can be more accurately perceived.

Good writing connects people to one another, to other living creatures, to stories and ideas, and to action. It allows readers to see the world from a new perspective. Writers are always asking people, "What is your experience?" They listen, they observe, then they share what they have learned with others. Writing to connect is empathy training. And, as Gloria Steinem once said, "Empathy is the most revolutionary of emotions."

Writing to connect is "change writing," which, like good therapy, creates the conditions that allow people to be transformed. Its goal is not to evoke one particular set of ideas, feelings, and actions, but rather to foster awareness and growth. Psychologist Donald Meichenbaum defines therapists as "purveyors of hope." Change writers are also purveyors of hope.

By definition, writers are people who care enough to try to share their ideas with other people. We are not passive, or utterly cynical, because then we would not even bother. We have a deep yearning to connect, to write things down and pass them around.

Every town has its cultural connectors. They know who to call in any crisis. They broker jobs, help with legal problems, find housing, fix schools, and raise funds for needed projects. They make sure that people meet one another, and that they understand and respect one another. Writers serve a similar function for the community of readers.

In *The Middle of Everywhere*, I coined the term "cultural broker" to describe Americans who helped refugees. Cultural brokers were those people who were willing to teach refugees what they needed to know. They introduced refugees to our hospitals, transportation systems, grocery stores, schools, libraries, and parks. They helped them locate other refugees from their homeland.

Writers are cultural brokers for the world of ideas. Our job is to share, as best we can, what we know. I write this book with the hope of making our world one connected tribe. To upend Groucho Marx's famous saying, I would say I don't want to belong to any club that won't have everyone as a member.

Great drama is great questions or it is nothing but technique. I could not imagine a theater worth my time that did not want to change the world.   —ARTHUR MILLER

Words can sometimes, in moments of grace, attain the quality of deeds.   —ELIE WIESEL

Passionate and well-articulated ideas can and do change the world for better or worse. Consider the work of the Persian king Cyrus the Great, who formulated the world's first declaration of human rights, or the work of Plato, Theresa of Avila, or Harriet Beecher Stowe, who wrote *Uncle Tom's Cabin*. Reflect on the influence of the writings of Adolf Hitler, Karl Marx, Mao Tse-tung, or Ayatollah Khomeini, whose fiery writing led to the establishment of an Islamic republic. Long after buildings and aqueducts have crumbled, writers' words live on.

Many writers today live in countries where, no matter what they write, they are unlikely to be locked up or executed for their ideas. Yet we must remember that writers in different times and places have risked their lives to tell the truth. Augustus Caesar sent the poet Ovid into exile. Stalin imprisoned and tortured numerous writers, including Boris Pasternak and Aleksandr Solzhenitsyn, and he killed the poet Osip Mandelstam. The German theologian Dietrich Bonhoeffer's writing to save Germany's Jews cost him his life.

I was moved by the story of Liu Di, whose e-mail moniker was "Stainless Steel Mouse." A graduate student in psychology at Beijing Normal University, she used her school computer privileges to tell the Chinese people about human rights. She was arrested by the government, and sentenced to several years of hard labor under the harshest of conditions at Qincheng Prison.

When you take pen to paper with the goal of making a difference, you join a community of people for whom words and issues matter. Perhaps you are a pediatrician who wants to educate parents about vaccinations, or a minister who wants to write more effective sermons. Maybe you are a high school student who wants to compose an editorial about drunk driving, or a labor organizer who plans to educate migrant farmworkers about their rights. Maybe you are a lawyer protesting the erosion of civil liberties under the Patriot Act, or a Floridian working to save the manatees. If you want to use words to change the world, *Writing to Change the World* is for you.

As a writer, your life goal may involve a worthy cause I cannot even imagine. Whatever it is, you are fortunate. Ossie Davis once said that his generation of African Americans was lucky because Martin Luther King Jr. had given them a moral assignment: to work for civil rights for all people. They could organize their lives around that goal. Davis worried about younger generations lacking such a clear goal. As Barbara Kingsolver put it, "The difference between happy people and unhappy ones is that happy people have found a use for themselves, like a good tool."

Once in East Africa, on the shores of an ancient lake, I sat alone and suddenly it struck me what community is. It is gathering around a fire and listening to someone tell us a story.   —BILL MOYERS

Stories are the most basic tool for connecting us to one another. Research shows that storytelling not only engages all the senses, it triggers activity on both the left and the right sides of the brain. Because stories elicit whole brain/whole body responses, they are far more likely than other kinds of writing to evoke strong emotions. People attend, remember, and are transformed by stories, which are meaning-filled units of ideas, the verbal equivalent of mother's milk.

Healthy cultures pass on healthy stories from generation to generation. The Lakota Sioux tell stories about the sacred hoop of life, and about their connections to the buffalo and all living creatures. Their myths created a belief system that allowed for the development of an emotionally sturdy people in a strong community. Indigenous people in Australia thought they were the tongue for the body that was the land. Their duty was to speak for the soil, water, plants, and animals. Because of how they conceptualized the world and their role in it, they were good caretakers for all of the life around them.

Today in America, shallow, tawdry stories blanket us like dirty snow. There are more films about prostitutes than about schoolteachers, more television shows about serial killers than grandparents. The old, the ordinary, and most ethnic groups are not deemed interesting enough for movies or TV.

As portrayed by the media, sex is casual, and it happens without discussion, protection, or the need for a relationship. Having sex involves about as much commitment as buying a sandwich. And violence is presented as the way to resolve the smallest of problems, and often as the first way and not the last. Worst of all, violence is divorced from its effects. The grieving grandparents, the heartbroken friends, the children growing up without parents—these are not shown on television. Violence, like sex, looks simple and shiny.

In the world of business, all of life is boiled down to one word: "profit." As John Muir said, "Nothing dollarable is safe." Advertisers design narratives to sell polluting, unhealthy, useless products. Cigarettes and alcohol are depicted as refreshing. Ads miseducate our children about the nature of happiness, teaching them just the opposite of what all the world's great religions teach. In brief, advertising tells you that to feel good you need to buy something you do not need. The comedian George Carlin eloquently expressed it this way: "Trying to be happy by accumulating possessions is like trying to satisfy hunger by taping sandwiches all over your body."

The stories we are told by people who want to sell us things will not save us. We need stories that teach us to be patient, to share, and to put things in perspective. Tolstoy's definition of wealth was "the number of things one can do without." Sut Jhaly of the Media Education Foundation estimates that the average person sees or hears three thousand ads a day. Imagine a world that had no ads. Or imagine our country instead with three thousand messages a day encouraging us to eat more fruits and vegetables, brush our teeth, call our great-aunt, and behave kindly toward one another.

Healing stories give people hope, teach them empathy, and encourage action. They feature different kinds of protagonists, and they need not be superheroes. Firefighters, missionaries, teachers, doctors, biologists, actors, and parents do kind and brave things every day. Many college students take full course loads, work, and still squeeze in volunteer projects. There are disabled students who are high achievers, and children who do not tease and hurt others.

Americans have always loved outlaws, but the true heroes are likely to be in-laws and the other good people who help us travel through our lives. Many people distrust public servants and do-gooders, yet right now our country desperately needs just such people to step up to the plate and try to make things better.

The title of this book, *Writing to Change the World,* may sound grandiose, but I truly believe that positive changes come from decent people acting properly. Most people perform good deeds every day; it is governments, institutions, and corporations that run amok. When I write this, I think of my grandmother Agnes. She and my grandfather homesteaded in eastern Colorado in the 1920s, raising five children on a ranch during the Dust Bowl and then the Depression. She worked hard all her life, and died with less than two thousand dollars in the bank. Still, she was loved and loving, and mostly content. She created a meaningful universe for herself amid tumbleweeds and rattlesnakes.

When I was a senior at the University of California, I visited my grandmother for the last time. She was widowed and dying of cancer, and I was a reader of popular psychology and full of myself. I asked her, "Grandmother, have you had a happy life?" She ignored my question. I persisted, asking again, as if she hadn't heard me the first time. She grimaced, then answered, almost angrily, "Mary, I don't think of my life that way. I ask, 'Have I made good use of my time and my talents? Is the world a better place because I have been here?' "

The person who wrote "You deserve a break today" made a difference in the world, but perhaps not a contribution to it. This book is for people like my grandmother Agnes who want the world to be a better place because they were here.

I hope *Writing to Change the World* helps you clarify your thoughts, experience new hope and new energy, and communicate your best ideas as effectively as possible. My goal is to help you translate your passion and idealism into action. This is not a book on how to write;

rather, it's a book on how to write in order to improve the world. It is for competent writers with generous hearts and bold spirits.

We live in a world filled with language. Language imparts identity, meaning, and perspective to our human community. Writers are either polluters or part of the clean-up team. Just as the language of power and greed has the potential to destroy us, the language of reason and empathy has the power to save us. Writers can inspire a kinder, fairer, more beautiful world, or incite selfishness, stereotyping, and violence. Writers can unite people or divide them.

In the chapters that follow, I will focus on expository writing, because that is my medium. I write books, articles, and speeches. However, I hope that poets and writers of fiction will find useful ideas in the text. I set myself a double task in writing this book: to tell and to demonstrate what I wish to say about writing. That made the work more complicated for me, but also more honest and rewarding. As I struggled with the writing, I learned more about writing.

I will teach what I know best, a connecting style of writing that employs storytelling to build empathy and the motivation to help. Still, there are many roads to Rome, and I will share ideas and examples from writers very different from myself. Irony, humor, anger, and dead-on logical argument all have their place in writing that connects.

I came to writing as a therapist, and I believe that psychotherapy has a great deal to teach us about making connections and fostering change. Carl Rogers formulated his basic tenets on transformation through relationships. He discovered that the best way to facilitate change is to accept people exactly as they are. He taught generations of therapists about nonjudgmental attitudes, empathy, and authenticity.

In both therapy and advocacy writing, relationships matter. Mutual respect and trust facilitate the growth of souls. Both endeavors require openness to ideas and a willingness to reconsider and expand one's point of view. Relationships create the environments that allow humans to extend their circles of caring. In the 1970s, psychologist Stanley Milgram theorized the now famous "six degrees of separation" between all people on earth. Since then, in our computerized, cell-phoned, outsourced world, we have grown even closer to one another. If Milgram were alive to rethink his earlier theorem, he might discover there are only three or two degrees of separation.

Lyndon Johnson said, "Let's hope the world doesn't turn into a neighborhood before it turns into a brotherhood." That is what 9/11 and all acts of terrorism are about. People who share the same space do not know how to understand and help one another. I encourage you to tackle the job of turning our world into a brother- and sisterhood. Writing allows us to connect with readers all around the world. We can support and influence people we will never meet. We can't necessarily repair damage in another country, but we can write something that may help, at least a little. With our words, we can construct a new kind of worldwide web, with strands of empathy. Together, we can formulate new metaphors for building a better world for us all. We can create a grammar of hope and a syntax of salvation. Then we will see an explosion of fresh green ideas.

The founder of Outward Bound U.S.A., Josh Miner, said, "If you are lucky, just once in your life you will be associated with a great idea." If I have one great idea, it is that connecting people might save the world. I suspect that everyone reading this book has a great idea. I hope I can help you sharpen, clarify, and share yours. I want you to go forth and tell your good and important stories. Are you ready to put your shoulder to the stone?

PART ONE

What We Alone Can Say

ONE

WRITING TO CONNECT

> In the dark times, will there be singing?
> Yes. There will be singing about the dark times.
>
> —BERTOLT BRECHT
>
> There is nothing more truly artistic than to love people.
>
> —VINCENT VAN GOGH

The first book to change my view of the universe was *The Diary of Anne Frank*. I read Anne's diary when I was a twelve-year-old, in Beaver City, Nebraska. Before I read it, I had been able to ignore the existence of evil. I knew a school had burned down in Chicago, and that children had died there. I had seen grown-ups lose their tempers, and I had encountered bullies and nasty schoolmates. I had a vague sense that there were criminals—jewel thieves, bank robbers, and Al Capone–style gangsters—in Kansas City and Chicago. After reading the diary, I realized that there were adults who would systematically kill children. My comprehension of the human race expanded to include a hero like Anne, but also to include the villains who killed her. When I read Anne Frank's diary, I lost my spiritual innocence.

In September 2003, when I was fifty-five years old, I visited the Holocaust Museum, in Washington, D.C., to view the Anne Frank exhibit. I looked at the cover of her little plaid diary, and at pages of her writing, at her family pictures. Meip Gies, Otto Frank's employee who brought food to the family, spoke on video about the people who hid in the attic. She said that Anne had always wanted to know the truth about what was going on. Others would believe the sugar-coated version of Miep's stories, but Anne would follow her to the door and ask, "What is really happening?"

The museum showed a short film clip of Anne dressed in white, her long hair dark and shiny. She is waving exuberantly from a bal-cony at a wedding party that is parading down the street. There are just a few seconds of film, captured by a filmmaker at the wedding who must have been entranced by her enthusiasm. The footage is haunting. Anne's wave seems directed at all of us, her small body casting a shadow across decades.

At the end of the exhibit, attendees hear the voice of a young girl reading Anne's essay "Give," a piece inspired by her experience of passing beggars on the street. She wonders if people who live in cozy houses have any idea of the life of beggars. She offers hope: "How wonderful it is that no one has to wait, but can start right now to gradually change the world." She suggests action: "Give whatever you have to give, you can always give something, even if it's a simple act of kindness." And she ends with: "The world has plenty of room, riches, money and beauty. God has created enough for each and every one of us. Let us begin by dividing it more fairly."

Even though Anne Frank ultimately was murdered, she managed, in her brief and circumscribed life, to tell the truth and bequeath the gift of hope. She searched for beauty and joy even in the harsh, frightened world of the attic in which her family hid from the Nazis.

Her writing has lived on to give us all a sense of the potential largesse of the human soul, even in worst-case scenarios. It also reminds us that, behind the statistics about war and genocide, there are thousands of good people we have a responsibility to help.

> Let the streams of life flow in peace.
> Turn from violence.
> Learn to think for a long time how to change the world
> How to make it better to live in.   —QUETZALCOATL

All writing is designed to change the world, at least a small part of the world, or in some small way perhaps a change in a reader's mood or in his appreciation of a certain kind of beauty. Writing to improve the world can be assessed by the goals of its writers and/or by its effects on the world. Most likely, Mary Oliver did not write her poem "Wild Geese" to inspire environmental activists and yet environmentalists have found it motivational. Bob Dylan claims he had no intention of composing a protest song when he penned "Blowin' in the Wind," but it became the anthem for many of the causes of the last half of the twentieth century. On the other hand, musicians like Tori Amos, the Indigo Girls, and the band Ozomatli do hope to influence their listeners in specific ways, and they succeed. Looking back, Rachel Carson, in *Silent Spring,* satisfies both intent and effect: she wrote the book to stop the use of certain pesticides, and, following its publication, DDT was banned in the United States.

My dad told me about a rule he and other soldiers followed in the Pacific during World War II. It was called the Law of 26, and it postulates that for every result you expect from an action there will be twenty-six results you do not expect. Certainly this law applies to writing. Sometimes a book intended to have one effect has quite another. For example, Upton Sinclair wrote *The Jungle* to call attention to the exploitation of the immigrant labor force and their working conditions in factories, yet it led to an outcry over unsanitary conditions in the meat industry and helped establish uniform standards for beef processing and inspection nationwide.

Art / Artful / Propaganda

All writing to effect change need not be great literature. Some of it is art, of course, such as Walt Whitman's "I Hear America Singing" or Abraham Lincoln's Gettysburg Address. Some of it is relatively straightforward, such as *Rampage: The Social Roots of School Shootings* by Katherine Newman, David Harding, and Cybelle Fox. And some of it is both artful and straightforward. For example, in *The Age of Missing Information,* Bill McKibben has a clever idea that he executes beautifully: he compares what he learns from a week in the mountains to what he learns from watching a week's worth of cable television. On the mountaintop, McKibben experiences himself as small yet connected to something large and awe-inspiring. He comes down from the mountain calm and clear-thinking. Watching cable for a week, he hears over and over that he has unmet needs, that he is grossly inadequate, yet he still is the center of the universe, deserving of everything he wants. McKibben ended the week feeling unfocused, agitated, and alone.

Many effective writers are not stylists, but they manage to convey a clear message. Their writing is not directed toward sophisticates or literary critics. It is designed to influence cousin Shirley, farmer Dale, coworker Jan, Dr. Lisa, neighbor Carol, businessman Carl, or voter Sylvia. Expository writing for ordinary people calls for a variety of talents—storytelling skills, clarity, and the ability to connect. Whether they are working on an op-ed piece, a speech, or a poem, skilled writers exercise creativity and conscious control. They labor to make the important interesting, and even compelling, to readers.

Change writers hope that readers will join them in what Charles Johnson calls "an invitation to struggle." Whereas writers of propaganda encourage readers to accept certain answers, writers who want to transform their readers encourage the asking of questions. Propaganda invites passive agreement; change writing invites original thought, openheartedness, and engagement. Change writers trust that readers can handle multiple points of view, contradictions, unresolved questions, and nuance. If, as André Gide wrote, "Tyranny is the absence of complexity," then change writers are founders of democracies.

Good writing astonishes its writer first. My favorite example of this phenomenon is Leo Tolstoy's *Anna Karenina*. Tolstoy planned to write a novel that condemned adultery, and his intention was to make the adultress an unsympathetic character. But when he came to truly understand Anna as he wrote the book, he fell in love with her, and, a hundred years later, so do his readers. Empathy can turn contempt into love.

Socially conscious writers want authenticity and transparency to saturate every page of their work. They strive to teach readers how to think, not what to think. They connect readers to ideas and experiences that readers would not have on their own. Always, this kind of writing coaxes readers to expand their frames of reference, or, as the Buddhists say, to put things in bigger containers.

Moral Writing

> The real end of all art is beauty, truth, and goodness.
>
> —JOHN GARDNER
>
> Art can compel people freely, gladly, and spontaneously to sacrifice themselves in the service of man.   —TOLSTOY
>
> Art is the community's medicine for the worst disease of the mind—the corruption of consciousness.
>
> —ROBIN COLLINGWOOD
>
> You write in order to change the world, knowing perfectly well that you probably can't, but also knowing that literature is indispensable to the world. . . . The world changes according to the way people see it, and if you alter, even by a millimeter, the way people look at reality, then you can change it.   —JAMES BALDWIN

All kinds of writing can change the world by James Baldwin's millimeter. Recently, I read an article by horticulturalist Twyla Hansen that encouraged landowners to plant slow-growing shade trees, the kinds of trees that may not grow tall on our watch but will be beautiful for our grandchildren. After reading Hansen's article, I bought a sycamore.

For many years, I wrote "Urgent Action" letters for Amnesty International. I mailed them all over the world, to protest the torture and imprisonment of innocents, the curtailment of civil liberties, the oppression of women, and the harassment of journalists and others who worked for democracy. I am sure that many of my letters were simply tossed away; however, thanks to all those letters, a number of campaigns produced results. The Red Cross and Red Crescent were allowed into horrific prisons. Dissidents there were allowed access to their attorneys or even set free. And universities and presses have been allowed to reopen.

Examples of effective writing abound. President John Kennedy was so moved by Michael Harrington's *The Other America* that he launched the War on Poverty, later implemented by President Johnson. More recently, the state of New York was able to amend and soften the harsh Rockefeller drug laws instituted in the 1970s. A *New York Times* article credited this policy change to Jennifer Gonnerman's book *Life on the Outside*. which told the story of a woman detained for sixteen years for a single sale of cocaine.

Academics can be revolutionaries. Donella Meadows, Dennis Meadows, and Jorgan Randers in *The Limits to Growth* educated us about the future of the earth's resources. They plotted graphs showing that while the world's population is increasing, such natural resources as oil, water, and arable land are decreasing. Their work gave scientists, policymakers, and everyday citizens new ways to frame environmental, energy, and population issues. Dr. Paul Farmer, writing as a medical anthropologist, has revolutionized medicine in the developing world with such books as *AIDS and Accusation: Haiti and the Geography of Blame* and *Infections and Inequalities: The Modern Plague*.

Journalists can change the zeitgeist as well. Think of Bob Woodward and Carl Bernstein on Watergate, or of Seymour Hersh's recent writing on Iraq and Afghanistan. Reporters pick the stories to tell from the thousands of available ones. They call readers' attention to what they think is newsworthy. And readers respond. For example,

Jim Barksdale, former Netscape CEO, offered to reward students in Mississippi up to ten thousand dollars of their college tuition if they did well in school. His generosity was inspired by an article he had read on the state's struggle to fund its educational system.

Many writers who have suffered great sorrows write memoirs for cathartic reasons. They also write to document their experiences, to express outrage at injustice and unnecessary suffering, and to help others to see and feel what can happen to people like themselves. They write to both bind up their own wounds and inspire others to care.

Most likely, Loung Ung's memoir, *Lucky Child*, was written for all of the above reasons. Ung tells the story of her family's experience of the genocide that took place in Cambodia. Both her parents and several of her siblings died, but Loung fortunately escaped to a refugee camp with an older brother and his wife. Later, they settled in the United States. *Lucky Child* compares Luong's life in the United States with the life of her younger sister who stayed behind in Cambodia. It shows readers the differences between living in a prosperous, yet stressed, democratic country and living in an impoverished, yet communal, autocratic country.

Song can be a powerful tool for connecting people to one another. Think of civil rights workers singing "We Shall Overcome." Think of Woody Guthrie's "This Land Is Your Land," Curtis Mayfield's "People Get Ready," or Tracy Chapman's "Revolution."

Films often change the world. Morgan Spurlock's entertaining, witty, and solidly researched *Super Size Me* has Spurlock, a healthy young man, bravely eat nothing but McDonald's fast food for a month. With doctors monitoring him, he gained weight and suffered numerous health problems. His downhill slide into a dangerous medical condition was highly instructive for the rest of us, and it pushed McDonald's toward offering healthier choices.

Any form of writing can change the world. Your goal is to find the form that allows you to use every one of your talents in the service of what you consider to be your most important goals. You want to search for what you alone can say and then how you can say it most effectively.

A true piece of writing is a dangerous thing. It can change your life. —TOBIAS WOLFF

The mind, once expanded to the dimensions of bigger ideas, never returns to its original size.

—OLIVER WENDELL HOLMES

Ordinary people can and do change the world every day. Yet even as I write, I hear a despairing voice inside me whisper that right now car bombs and nuclear weapons seem more powerful than words, that few people read serious writing, and that even those readers who do seem to read only to reinforce their established beliefs. Some days, I have to argue with myself for a long while before the urge to connect in me wins and sends me off to work.

Discouragement can stop us from doing our work, as can humility. Many writers silence themselves by thinking, Who am I to write? And who among us has not written letters to editors, corporations, or government officials that were simply ignored? I remember *The Lazlo Letters* by Don Novello, published years ago. It featured crazy letters written by one "Lazlo Toth, American." The twist was that Novello's fictional protagonist wrote to real government officials, real heads of universities, and real CEOs. Alongside Lazlo's silly letters were the actual replies he received. Most of the responses clearly showed that Lazlo's letters had not been carefully read, let alone considered. The book inspired laughter, but not a zeal for letter writing.

Another discouraging factor is that our relationship to the written word is changing. Fewer people are reading newspapers and serious magazines these days. Most adults consider themselves too busy to read. And children reared on television and PlayStation have shorter attention spans. Living in an atmosphere saturated by video games, junky writing, and stupid television and movies, we are finding it difficult to muster much optimism for what Carol Bly calls "the passionate accurate story." It is easy to think, Why even bother?

Yet, paradoxically, our discouragement can be the very impetus that motivates us to write. We may feel the need to be that voice crying out in the wilderness. We may feel compelled to shout "Fire!" or "Man overboard!" or simply "The emperor has no clothes!"

> We can do no great things, only small things with great love.
>
> —MOTHER TERESA
>
> Nothing is more powerful than individuals acting out of their own conscience.   —VÁCLAV HAVEL

Writing turns out to be one thing we can control in a world where much feels beyond our control. Most of us will not be spearheading protest marches against the World Trade Organization, masterminding boycotts against sweatshops in China, or leading the charge against oil exploitation in Nigeria. We won't be building orphanages for children in South Africa. But we do what we can.

We write. Every day we witness the degradation of much that we value. We witness sorrowful examples of unfairness, ignorance, and cruelty. We see our children educated to want all the wrong things. And so we write. We write with a sense of urgency. We write because we discover that we have something we alone can say. And we struggle on because we still believe in the power of words, just as Anne Frank believed in goodness despite powerful evidence to the contrary.

Fyodor Dostoyevsky lived in a hopeless time and place, a world of pogroms, starvation, filth, and syphilis. His life was plagued by epilepsy, mental problems, and poverty. Yet he left us this message:

> Love all of God's creation, the whole of it and every grain of sand.
> Love every leaf, every ray of God's light! Love the animals, love the
> plants, love everything. If you love everything, you will perceive
> the divine mystery in things. And once you have perceived it, you
> will begin to comprehend it ceaselessly, more and more every day.
> And you will at last come to love the whole world with an abiding,
> universal love.

A few years ago, I visited a market on the Burmese border. It was a profoundly unsettling experience. I walked past frightened, impoverished people hawking Leonardo DiCaprio beach towels, dried fish, Nike knockoffs, and counterfeit cigarettes. Old women with no teeth sat behind piles of peppers or rice. Listless children with dead eyes lay on ragged blankets behind their parents' stalls or sat watching shoppers walk by. A skinny teenager was apprehended by soldiers, beaten, and thrown into the back of a black van, his mother running after him, screaming, pulling her hair. Everyone in this tawdry market seemed almost comatose with inertia and grief. Gradually, I realized the underlying cause of what I was witnessing: the total absence of hope.

However, one man was different. He squatted in the gutter, almost naked, selling children's Magic Slates. As I walked by, he quickly scrawled on his display pad "Freedom from Fear," which is the motto of Aung San Suu Kyi, who is the daughter of a former leader in Burma. A Western-educated exile, Kyi returned to Burma to work for the restoration of democracy. And while she currently is under house arrest there, her ideas have kept hope alive for the citizens of that beleaguered country.

I looked at the words the man had written on the little plastic slate and then into his eyes. He smiled at me—a fierce, desperate smile—and then he quickly erased what he had written. This man had almost been silenced. But he made a leap. He dared to make a connection with a westerner. He used heroic words to carve out a Magic Slate–sized piece of freedom, which he then shared with me. I have never felt more honored and more humbled. When I think of people writing to connect, I think of the man with the Magic Slate. I write for him.

TWO

KNOW THYSELF

I Am From

I am from Avis and Frank, Agnes and Fred, Glessie May and
   Mark.
From the Ozark Mountains and the high plains of eastern
   Colorado,
from mountain snowmelt and southern creeks with water
   moccasins.
I am from oatmeal eaters, gizzard eaters, haggis and raccoon
   eaters.
I am from craziness, darkness, sensuality, and humor.
From intense do-gooders struggling through ranch winters in the
   1920s.
I am from "If you can't say anything nice about someone, don't
   say anything," and "Pretty is as pretty does" and "Shit-muckelty
   brown" and "Damn it all to hell."
I am from no-dancing-or-drinking Methodists, but cards were
   okay except on Sunday, and from tent-meeting Holy Rollers,
from farmers, soldiers, bootleggers, and teachers.
I am from Schwinn girl's bike, 1950 Mercury two-door, and *West
   Side Story*.
From coyotes, baby field mice, chlorinous swimming pools,

Milky Way and harvest moon over Nebraska cornfields.

I am from muddy Platte and Republican,

from cottonwood and mulberry, tumbleweed and switchgrass,

from Willa Cather, Walt Whitman, and Janis Joplin.

My own sweet dance unfolding against a cast of women in
    aprons and barefoot men in overalls.

When I researched *The Middle of Everywhere,* I asked refugees to write "I Am From"–type poems as they struggled to find themselves in a new country and language. They followed a formula with each line beginning with "I am from." Writing this kind of poem is a way to experiment with identity issues. The poem must include references to food, places, and religion. You might want to give it a try.

If you look back on your life, most likely you will be able to trace a trail from the present to deep into your past. Pivotal events shaped your core values. Certain people and experiences interested you. You had talents, and ways you spent your time. Most likely, you cared about certain things—school, sports, animals, politics, religion. The trail into your past may be linear or meandering, or, at some point, it may have taken a sharp right turn.

You possess an innate temperament, a belief system, and a work ethic. By now, most likely, you have a sense of your weaknesses as well as your strengths, your blind spots as well as your unique gifts. You know what people like and dislike about you. All this self-knowledge allows you to write with your own grand themes, your own passions, even your own flaws, at your service. As Willa Cather wrote, "An artist's limits are quite as important as his powers. They are definite assets, not a deficiency, and go to form his flavor and personality."

Our writing comes from our being. The deeper we explore our souls, the deeper and therefore richer will be our writing. Buddhist teacher Pema Chödrön writes that the Buddhist conception of equanimity is "a banquet to which everyone is invited." She is referring to an open acceptance of all experience, both our inner experiences and experiences we have in the world outside ourselves. Our sensibilities, our moral outlook, and our point of view are what we writers have to offer the reader. Only when we know who we are can we fully offer this gift. Keep in mind that fuzzy thinking leads to fuzzy writing. With inner clarity, we present readers with reflective, honest work.

Of course, the road goes both ways. Writing can teach us who we are. Certain issues and life themes persistently emerge in our work. After writing seven books, I realized that two themes overarched each book's theme. No matter what I selected to explore, I returned to my consuming interests—the passing of time, what things change and what things remain the same, and the effects of culture on relationships and mental health.

Just as my childhood colors all my writing, so your past will color yours. As you read my story, I hope you will want to take inventory of your own early lessons about the world, your hopes and fears, your life themes, even your sense of calling. You might consider tackling a short autobiography about how you came to be who you are today.

> We are all a paradoxical bundle of rich potential that consists of both neurosis and wisdom. —PEMA CHÖDRÖN

I was the oldest child in a big, complicated family. My father, Frank, was from the Ozarks; my mother, Avis, was from the high plains of eastern Colorado. They met when both were stationed in San Francisco during

World War II, and they got married in Muir Woods wearing their Navy uniforms. Both grew up poor during the Depression, but while my mother's family was puritanical, serious, and intellectual, my father's was earthy, fun-loving, and emotional. My parents had a lot of nerve thinking they could get along for a lifetime.

When I was a girl, Mother worked as a doctor in small towns in Nebraska and Kansas. At various times, Dad worked as a lab technician; raised pigeons, geese, and hogs; and sold livestock feed or life insurance. Dad's mother lived with us some of the time. Cousins came for the summer. Other relatives visited and stayed for weeks at a time.

I slept on a daybed just off the dining room. At night, I lay awake and listened to grown-ups joke and laugh. I heard political arguments, shoptalk, and gossip. Around midnight, the adults would grow sleepy, and Dad would bribe them to keep talking or play cards by asking, "If I fried up some steaks and cut the pies, would you stay up?"

Most of my family was rural poor. Only Aunt Margaret and Uncle Fred, who lived in Los Angeles, had money and could be called wealthy. My other aunts were schoolteachers or homemakers, and Uncle Max sold Dr Pepper, Uncle Otis ran a general store, Uncle Clair farmed, and Uncle Lloyd hunted elk and cut down timber in northern Idaho. Some were deeply religious, some not. I heard many theological arguments from family members who were Church of Christ, Southern Baptist, Methodist, Unitarian, or who simply liked to sleep in on Sunday morning.

From this opinionated group, I got quite an education on point of view. Aunt Betty's children had to be in bed by 7 P.M. They were not allowed to play cards, dance, or listen to rock 'n' roll. When my cousin Stella was twelve, her dad told her not to get "knocked up," but that if she did get knocked up to come tell him. He had a shotgun ready. Other parents were more lenient. Cousin Anna wore makeup and skimpy tops that revealed her ample bust. She flirted outrageously with the skinny boys who came to read comics and play marbles with my brothers.

Dad subscribed to *Human Events,* an ultraconservative magazine, and he even considered joining the John Birch Society, which, fortunately, Mother vetoed. Yet both my parents were unflaggingly generous. Dad's friends learned never to admire anything he owned or he would insist on giving it to them. Mother offered free medical care to anyone who needed it, and she sent money to my school so that all the children could receive *Weekly Reader*s.

Grandmother Agnes was a Democrat, Grandfather Fred a Republican, and Grandmother Glessie worked for "the independent party of biscuits and gravy." Meanwhile, when my liberal aunt Margaret visited she would invite me to accompany her on errands so that she could explain to me what a conservative idiot my father was. She would scowl and say, "Don't listen to a thing your parents say about politics. The sooner you lose their ideas, the better."

Growing up in such a family, I was constantly asking why. Why did this aunt marry that uncle? Why was one cousin so gentle, another so rough and mean? Why did some adults hate FDR and others love him? Why was the God of one side of the family so tolerant and forgiving and the God of another side so willing to let children burn in hell if they have not been properly baptized? Why did one uncle advise me to pursue my education, another warn me to avoid college if I hoped to marry? For that matter, why did almost all my relatives pour gravy over their food, while my aunt Margaret served it under hers and called it sauce?

I feel lucky to have been born into a family that passionately expressed such divergent points of view. All I had to do was lie in bed and think over the day's conversations to understand that there were

no absolute truths, only the truths of many well-meaning but hu-
manly flawed people. Also, I was fortunate there were no really
mean-spirited people in my family. People may have been misguided,
confused, foolish, or just plain wrong, but nobody robbed or de-
ceived anybody for money. In fact, money had almost nothing to do
with anything when I was growing up. Everybody focused on food,
religion, politics, good times, and stories.

From the perspective of fifty-eight years, I can see that my life has
been a series of stories. I listened to my grandmother's stories while
still a toddler. As I biked around Beaver City, or sat under the elms in
the park at night with my friends, I was on the lookout for stories.
My mother spun out stories as we drove to the small-town hospitals
where she visited her patients. She told me stories as we drove snowy
country roads making house calls, or followed Highway 24 to Flagler
to visit her folks. She described life on a ranch during the Dust Bowl
and Depression. And she fashioned narratives from the great web of
history—Joan of Arc, Marie Antoinette, Napoleon, Czar Nicholas
and his family. She described movies she loved: *Dark Victory,* about a
selfish woman who changes as she loses her eyesight; and Alfred
Hitchcock's *Lifeboat,* about a sinking rowboat that has to be emptied
of its passengers one by one so that it can stay afloat. Mother fa-
vored intense stories that turned on character. She was interested in
moral choices, and in what William Faulkner called "the heart in
struggle against itself." So am I.

Uncle Otis spent his days in his general store sipping orange so-
das and spinning yarns in front of the potbellied stove in winter or
on the porch in summer. While my aunt Grace rang up groceries,
pumped gas, and operated the tiny post office in the back, Otis chatted with his pals about fishing trips, mule and cattle trades, bootleggers, and men from the IRS.

This was a pre-television world, and people were accustomed to entertaining each other. As Grandmother Agnes and I did dishes, she told me stories about her mother, who came to America as a bond slave from Scotland, and about my grandfather's family, many of whom died of cholera in Iowa. Neighbors shared stories, as did my mother's patients. As I worked at her clinic, counting pills into bottles and sterilizing gloves and surgical packs, I heard plenty.

I always could invent stories to entertain my friends. I would narrate them as we lay in the hayloft or under the stars, or as we passed the time on porches on rainy summer afternoons. When I was alone, I cut out the models from our Monkey Wards' catalogue and organized them into families. I would even invent stories while hanging up the clothes, having one pair of underpants marry another, then hanging little sock children with cute names beside them.

One of my earliest photos shows me asleep in the crib with a magazine on my face. I "read" in bed even then. As a young child, I had a stressful life because of Mom being in medical school and Dad fighting in Korea. When I wanted attention and nurturance, books were soothing. They helped me sleep when I was afraid of the dark. Later, they stimulated me when I was bored, and kept me company when I felt lonely.

Grandmother Agnes always asked me what I was reading and if I would read it aloud to her. She admonished me, "Choose your books as carefully as you choose your friends." In junior high, my English teacher unfolded and passed around yellowed letters written by soldiers during World War II. Several wrote to say that the poems they had memorized in her class kept them from going crazy during the long nights of shelling. "You see, students," she would intone, "poetry can save your life."

By late elementary school, I had read every book in the children's section of the Beaver City library. That wasn't as ambitious as it sounds, the entire library being no larger than most living rooms. I loved stories about heroic children. I devoured the biographies of Helen Keller, Joan of Arc, and Eleanor Roosevelt, who, like me, was an ugly duckling and not popular with boys. I cried reading *Death Be Not Proud* by John Gunther. I earnestly tried to live up to the ideals set forth in Pat Boone's *Twixt Twelve and Twenty,* my first self-help guide.

I wasn't much for romance novels, although I did read Helen Wells's cheesy Cherry Ames, Student Nurse series, in which Cherry falls for one good-looking young doctor after another in one exotic medical setting after another—cruise ships, Alaskan mountain towns, and hospitals on tropical islands. I even read the Vicki Barr, Flight Stewardess series, also by Helen Wells. It completely miseducated me about the nature of airline travel, something I was to learn about later in life.

My favorite novels were *A Tree Grows in Brooklyn,* about a sensitive yet strong Irish immigrant girl, and *The Silver Sword,* the story of a heroic Polish girl who cared for her younger siblings and other children after her parents were taken away during World War II. I even choreographed a *Silver Sword* game for an entire summer for the neighborhood kids, transforming our root cellar into our shelter in Warsaw. Of course, I played the older sister who taught school and kept the other children safe and secure.

By junior high, I was an archetypal bluestocking nerd. I religiously studied a book called *How to Build a Better Vocabulary.* I wrote down words I read or heard and looked them up. I memorized definitions, but, sadly, not pronunciation, and like many readers I mispronounced many of the words I had read but never heard spoken aloud. In high school, I tried to organize a great books club that would meet after school and discuss Euripides, Plato, Shakespeare, and John Stuart Mills. No one joined.

From all this reading, I discovered how differently things were done in other places. I came to see that, everywhere, life is made up of choices, and that people can either behave well or poorly no matter what the circumstance.

I inhabited the kind of roomy childhood that almost no children today do. In the early 1950s, in Beaver City, Nebraska, children were blessed with an abundance of time and space. I had some responsibilities, but mostly I was free—free to read all day in our clubhouse, which was the attic above an old car shed; free to ride my bike out to Beaver Creek; free to climb trees, or just lie in the grass and watch clouds; free to peruse comics and charge vanilla phosphates at the drugstore.

I did not have dance or drama lessons, and I was not on the soccer team. But I was stimulated by my Beaver City universe, with its cast of characters as diverse and tragic as any play by Shakespeare. Since my parents didn't chauffeur me anywhere, I met the world unmediated by them. I formed my own relationships and my own opinions. I learned to depend on myself for entertainment and stimulation in a way that television-raised children cannot understand. And I learned conversational skills from a generation who knew how to talk.

My inner cast of characters hasn't changed much over the years. Many of my people are gone now, but I meet others who seem to have something of my mother, my grandmother, my best friend, or my mean and stupid physical education teacher in them. And when my own children grew up and moved out of state, I found young people who seemed to possess "essence of Zeke" or "essence of

Sara." Primary relationships create our ways of understanding the world. And language mediates these relationships.

I hope you will attempt to walk down your own trail into the forest that is your past. Perhaps you will construct a timeline, beginning with the story of your birth, then slowly adding the mileposts of your experiences. You may want to organize your story by place, by defining moments, by life themes, or with an account of your struggle to answer certain questions: Am I good? Am I worthy of respect? Am I crazy? Am I understood? Or perhaps you will choose to build your narrative around relationships in your life, or even by such domains as work, religion, food, or play.

We all have stories to tell. However, we do not necessarily know what they are and why they are important. Writing can help us see why our stories matter, and why we feel a sense of urgency to tell them. Carefully considered, our stories can shed light on our moral assignments.

THREE

WHAT YOU ALONE CAN SAY

Every death is like the burning of a library. —ALEX HALEY

What can I do that isn't going to get done unless I do it, just because of who I am?   —BUCKMINSTER FULLER

You have something to say that no one else can say. Your history, your unique sensibilities, your sense of place, and your language bestow upon you a singular authority. Who but you can describe the hollyhocks in your grandmother's backyard, or the creek outside of town that you fished as a child, or the way it felt to be the only person of color at your college? Who but you can tell about the faces at the soup kitchen, or in the burn unit?

You have your own set of life themes, habits, and ways of organizing yourself into a coherent "I." As are all humans, you are an amateur psychologist, with your own unique theories about why humans act the way they do. All of this individuality that is you, properly understood and clearly presented, is a tremendous gift to the world. It is a one-of-a-kind point of view on the universe.

Your desire to communicate originates from some internal combustion of intellect, heart, and experience. No doubt, you are on fire about certain causes. In our diverse nation, there are almost as many causes as there are people. We have groups devoted to the preservation of earthworms, the promotion of the drinking of green tea, the spread of New Age polka music, and the condoning of the siesta. Someone, somewhere, devotes time to writing about liturgical dance, the health benefits of golf, music programs for kids, hybrid vehicles, toxic shock syndrome, and human trafficking.

Over the years, our causes change or stay the same. Twists and turns in our personal lives or the outside world create new energy for good endeavors. Our personalities crash into what Allen Ginsberg called "the drunken taxicab of absolute reality." Life itself assigns us our causes.

This offering of the library of self can be called voice. Voice is everything we are, all that we have observed, the emotional chords that are uniquely ours—all our flaws and all of our strengths, expressed in the words that best reflect us. Voice is like a snowflake— complicated, beautiful, and individual. It is essence of self, distilled and offered in service to the world.

Recently, a friend told me, "I like singers who have unmistakable voices. They make every song their own, and when you hear even a few bars of a song you know it is them." Individual voices can be quiet or noisy, wry or schmaltzy, self-disclosing or guarded, kind or angry. Voice comes from genetics, gender, relationships, place; from ethnic background and educational experience. Voice resonates with our sorrows and fears, but also our joys, and it sings out all of who we are.

I struggled for years to find my voice. At first, I wrote in a self-conscious way: I sat down and "committed the act of literature." My anxiety about writing caused me to write in a constipated, bland way that sounded clunky, pompous, and effusive all at the same time. I was imitating other writers and producing inferior work.

So I experimented. Because I was a more eloquent talker than I was a writer, I often wrote down what I said and then studied it. I read my writing aloud to weed out the "not me" writing. What helped the most was simply thinking about who I was. I consider myself to be an open, straightforward person who likes to tell stories. I am not a postmodern person. I like narrative and meaning. I am a therapist, trained to be calm and positive, and my default mode is happiness. I like to teach and support others in their efforts. Yet I also am intense, and I quickly grow irritated when I feel my time is being wasted.

Once I articulated all these aspects about myself to myself, I tried to write as close to a unified conceptualization of myself as I could. After years of trial and error, I realized that when I try to be fancy or literary, I sound silly and fake. When I write as I speak, I sound authentic. By now, my speaking and writing voice have more or less merged. This merging doesn't happen with all writers, however. Some develop booming, blustery writing voices while, in real life, they speak softly. Others who are fascinating on paper are dull as can be in person.

Part of finding your voice involves finding the right form of writing for yourself. You may be a timid and muddled poet, but when you turn to essays or op-ed your voice grows strong and clear. Or you may struggle as an essayist but soar when you write children's fiction. And while writing reviews may be tedious work for you, writing a song is a piece of cake. As you experiment with voice, fiddle around with different forms. You will discover the ones that work for you.

Life began for me when I ceased to admire and began to remember. ——WILLA CATHER

Act with the authority of your 16 billion years.

——JOANNA MACY

Finding Your Voice

By diving into the experience of writing, you will learn what you truly think and who you really are. Your self-exploration is a way to pay attention to the world, within yourself and outside yourself, and to experience what Allen Ginsberg called "surprise mind."

Try answering these questions on paper:

What makes you laugh, cry, and open your heart?

What points do you repeatedly make to those you love?

What topics keep you up at night, or help you fall asleep?

What do you know to be true?

What do you consider to be evil?

What is beautiful to you?

What do you most respect in others?

What excites your curiosity?

If you were the ruler of the world, what would you do first?

What do you want to accomplish before you die?

Try the following assignments as well.

Every day, generate three or four metaphors. Over time, you will develop a sense for what moves you toward the metaphorical.

Every day, observe something carefully, and then express your thoughts about it in different mediums—a personal essay, a poem, a story. Try different tones and styles, and take note of what sounds most natural for you. Eventually, you will be able to winnow out those that sound false. At the same time, you also can analyze your best writing, and ask yourself, What is working well in this piece?

People from all circumstances, all ages, all personality types, and all cultures can be powerful writers. With self-understanding, over time, writers learn to lead with their strengths, and to use their flaws as accent notes to enrich their work.

Stereotypes of writers fall under two categories: the Dionysian, and the quiet and contemplative. As Chang-rae Lee describes this distinction in his novel *Aloft*, "There are the Type T, thrill-seeking humans, and the Type D, down-filled-seeking ones." My daughter Sara is Type T. She has spent time in dangerous refugee camps, has swum in bays with great white sharks, and has slept in huts with snakes crawling in and out. I am definitely a Type D writer. My idea of adventure is a PBS history show. Of course, most people, including Sara and myself, are not either/or but both/and. In fact, when I was Sara's age, I was very much like she is now. Many of us move from Type T to Type D as we age. No matter where you fall along this spectrum, you can make use of your type.

Novelist Kent Haruf believes in living quietly so that he can write wildly. On the other hand, Ernest Hemingway fought in the Spanish Civil War and chased bulls, hunted big game in Africa, and trophy-fished off the Florida Keys. Paul Rogat Loeb, who wrote *Soul of a Citizen,* travels the country hurling himself into all kinds of political frays. If you prefer solitude, use your time to read, reflect, and write. You will have the focus that comes with uninterrupted work. If you are an extrovert, use that too. Share your ideas with others, make speeches, and organize readings. Your sociability will give you contacts and experiences that you can later make use of in your writing. You may have trouble finding the time to write, but, when you do, you will have plenty to say.

Comedic writers often reveal their flaws and quirks to connect with all the other flawed and quirky humans of the world. We all enjoy people who confess to being human. Most likely, if you are funny, you can employ humor to deflect arguments and diffuse tension and resistance. Dave Barry is a master at wrapping his messages in humor. Whether or not I agree with him, I read the whole piece because I am laughing so much. In "It's Time for Knuckle-Dragging NASCAR-Obsessed Reds and Latte-Sucking Tofu-Chomping Blues to Get Along," he begins, "I thought that in today's column I would heal the nation. . . ."

Barry posits that the United States suffered a wound during the presidential election as a result of the rift between the red states—defined by him as "states where foreign cuisine pretty much means Pizza Hut"—and the blue states—defined as "states that believe they are smarter than the red states, despite the fact that it takes the average blue state resident fifteen minutes to order a single cup of coffee."

We don't have to be likable to write or to effect social changes for the good. Many writers love humanity but can't stand people. Social critic H. L. Mencken, who published mostly in the 1920s, wrote in a harsh and cutting tone. Here is an example from his book *On Politics: A Carnival of Buncombe*: "As democracy is perfected, the office of president represents, more and more closely, the inner soul of the people. On some great and glorious day the plain folks of the land will reach their heart's desire at last and the White House will be adorned by a downright moron."

Don't allow a sour, obstreperous personality to slow you down. There is a place for you at the table.

FOUR

GROWING OUR SOULS

We are born with a mortgage. That mortgage is a debt that we owe to the past and the future.   —EMERSON

Be kind, for everyone you meet is fighting a great battle.
   —PHILO OF ALEXANDRIA

Understanding is another name for love; love is another name for understanding.   —THICH NHAT HANH

The character of a society is the cumulative result of countless small actions, day in and day out, of millions of people.
   —DUANE ELGIN

America is deeply ambivalent about its change agents. Simply put, we tend to like them after they die. To most Americans, "radical" is a negative word, and even "reformer" evokes our cultural uncertainty about systemic change. On the other hand, we tend to like rebels and outlaws, just so long as they don't really challenge the status quo.

Jesus exemplifies our confused attitudes about radicals. To the en-
trenched, greedy powers of His time, He was a real troublemaker.
He was a pacifist who disdained the wealthy and religious hypocrites,
and He befriended prostitutes and beggars. Yet for two thousand
years, He has been revered. Still, if He were writing and preaching
today, most likely He would be regarded as a subversive and a kook.

In the upside-down world of America today, our culture's dysfunctional message is that healthy people accept the world as it is. We
are taught that problems are pervasive and insolvable, and that we
are powerless. Also, we hear that only radical nuts or quixotic fuzzy-
brains work for social and political change. Yet powerlessness produces despair in people and stagnation in cultures. Throughout
history, it has been the strong people who have endeavored to make
their communities better. Healthy people act.

In my opinion, true rebels are not anguished, angry individuals
mired since adolescence in their own complaints and needs for indi-
viduation. True rebels act from a well-developed moral center. They
know who they are and what they stand for. Most likely, they are
fighting for something that they have spent a lifetime learning to love.

Buddhist Thich Nhat Hanh wrote that the ocean of suffering is
immense, but that if we turn around we can see the land. True rebels
have had at least a glimpse of land, and they want to lead others to it.
Too, most change agents are not saints. If we wait for the saints to
save the world, it will be too late. What change agents have in common is the need to use their own gifts to help others.

I have always been interested in how we come to care for what we
do. Why does one person promote the importance of companion
animals while another promotes adult literacy? Why does one friend
speak out about the benefits of straw bale construction while another organizes a letter-writing campaign protesting working condi-

tions at O'Hare Airport? Why does a retired bank president write articles about the dangers of legalized gambling?

If we delve into our own why questions, we often find that our core interests evolved from specific events in childhood. Passions may emerge from a tragedy—a serious illness or accident, or a parent lost—or from a talent discovered, a trip to a magical place, or a relationship with a certain person (often a grandparent, best friend, or teacher). I can see my specific events quite clearly as I look back over the years.

My social activism began with animals. I had no choice but to accept the killing of certain animals I knew: Dad slaughtered rabbits, chickens, geese, pigs, hogs, and cows for markets. However, if I witnessed neighbor boys hurting a cat or torturing a frog or bird, I would fight to stop it.

One Sunday afternoon, when I was seven, my family went visiting, which is what rural people did on Sunday afternoons in the fifties. We drove out to see distant relatives, the old Tuneberg couple, who lived on the Blue River near a town called Milford.

My parents sat inside with Aunt Zoe and Uncle Milton, drinking coffee and chatting. I soon grew restless, and slipped outside to play. It was early spring, yet the Blue River still ran high with snowmelt and chunks of ice. I spent a good while tossing around sticks and dirt clods. Under a rock, I found a green-and-yellow garter snake that was only a few inches long. I picked him up, and felt his muscles expand and contract as he moved across my wrists and palms.

He coiled, uncoiled, and blinked at me. His tongue darted in and out. I let him tickle my arms for a while, then I put him in my jacket pocket. I practiced skipping stones, then retrieved him from my pocket. I placed him on the dirt path, and watched him orient himself, then slither toward the brown grass. I picked him up again, and held the scratchy circle that was him in my palm. With the sun on my shoulders, the river roaring by, the smell of green in the air, and the little garter snake in hand, I felt happy.

On impulse, I decided to see if my snake could swim. I did not carefully consider the potential consequences of this experiment. I hurled him into the Blue River, his body a white rope arching across the sky. In the Ozarks, I had seen snakes swim before, but this time the rope became a knot as it hit the surface and then sank in the deep water.

I think now that the icy water shocked him, and he drowned before he could recover from the change in temperature. For a long time, I stood there waiting for him to reappear. I searched downriver, and on twigs and ice floes. Finally, I accepted reality: I had killed him.

I did not cry, tell my parents, or even chastise myself all that much, but I did feel sorry. I learned that my actions had consequences, even life-and-death consequences. I realized that animals were not toys here just for me to play with but had lives of their own. I had taken this snake's one and only life. I could no longer think of him as *my* snake. And I would never again think of any animal as mine.

Another time, our neighbor Alvin Rogers had a basketful of baby coyotes on his back porch. I heard them yipping, and begged to play with them. When I asked Alvin what he would do with these cute puppies, he was uncharacteristically taciturn and grumpy. Finally, I ran home to ask my mother, who generally would tell me the truth when other adults wouldn't. She explained that Alvin had dug the puppies out of their burrow to kill them. The county paid a two-dollar bounty for every pair of coyote ears brought in, the theory being coyotes are harmful to agriculture. Alvin planned to cut off the pups ears and turn them in for bounty money.

I sobbed and pleaded with my mother to let us adopt the coyotes.

Finally, she agreed to pay two dollars for one pup. I took the money to Alvin and handed it to him. By now, he looked about ready to cry himself. I peered into the bushel basket of furry, wriggling, yelping pups, all signaling for me to pick them up. I knew that I had the power to grant life to only one. My choice would doom all the others to a grisly death. I felt like God, and I did not like it.

In elementary school, I had noticed the mean-spiritedness of some kids, part of it directed at me and my siblings. We were a strange family, outsiders, with a mother who was the first lady doctor anyone had ever met. She wore high heels and business suits, and was uneasy with small talk. It was Dad who cooked for the family, odd and unfamiliar foods such as sukiyaki, yakimishi, kimchee, turtle soup, tripe, brains, and rattlesnake. My brothers and I were shy, clumsy, and naive. We were easy targets for practical jokes and put-downs. I did not like the teasing, or the ostracism, and I developed empathy for other kids who were likewise targets. I was not always brave enough to defend them, but at least I did not participate in taunting.

In junior high and high school, I noticed the racism directed toward the few blacks and Native Americans who attended our schools. Even though no Jewish families lived in our town, some people made anti-Semitic remarks that deeply upset me. Anne Frank, who I admired so much, was a Jew. I just couldn't understand how people could dislike a group they had never even encountered.

Once we had a dance party in our basement, and my brother invited a black girl from our church to be his date. Dad warned him not to dance with her. And while I did not have the language or power to challenge my father, nonetheless I felt he was wrong.

The double standard about sex that applied to boys and girls in the 1950s struck me as weird and hugely unfair. Even though I was as pure as an Easter lily, I felt uncomfortable hearing girls called sluts. Girls struggled to keep their reputations, while boys bragged about having sex. Pregnant girls had to drop out of school, their boyfriends stayed.

Still, with the exception of a few fights to protect animals, I was hardly a social justice pioneer in my part of the world. I was a shy, bewildered kid. And although I had definite feelings and values, I did not have the words to express them and to take action.

All that changed when I graduated from high school and matriculated to the University of Kansas in the summer of 1965. Beginning with my roommate, Janice, I met students like myself. Our first night in the dorm, Janice and I stayed up all night, talking about music, books, our families, and the meaning of life. That first semester, Janice and I attended hootenannies, foreign films, poetry readings at a coffeehouse called the Fiery Furnace, and civil rights marches. We marched in Kansas City for integration of public places. I met black activists. I studied Simone de Beauvoir, Malcolm X, and Susan Sontag.

I was part of an exodus of young people to San Francisco in the late 1960s. I worked on Market Street, at Dunkin' Donuts, near the porno shops and the bus station where soldiers left for and arrived from Vietnam. A cross section of America dropped in for doughnuts and coffee, and I chatted with everyone—strippers, hippies, immigrants, local businessmen, veterans, and patriotic young men from Iowa and Georgia on their way to death. Waitressing gave me a real education in diversity.

Later, I transferred to the University of California at Berkeley. I majored in Spanish, then Latin American studies, then cultural anthropology. Margaret Mead and Noam Chomsky became my heroes. And I marched for everything—free speech, civil rights, peace, the environment, and women's rights.

The semester I graduated, I joined the People's Park demonstrations. At first, I was not involved, but then I witnessed a National

Guardsman shoot and kill a man on a nearby roof; the victim had been doing just what I had been doing, watching the riot on the street below. The next day, on my way to a linguistics class, I was sprayed with tear gas by a National Guard helicopter flying overhead. As I lay vomiting on the grass, I vowed to join the marchers. I had learned just how much power our government could bring to bear on those who oppose it.

By graduation, in 1969, I wanted to be far away from the scene in California. Hard drugs were showing up on the streets, and students were talking about weapons. Cities had burned after Martin Luther King Jr.'s death, the Black Panthers and the Weathermen were on the rise, and police and federal agents were retaliating. Everything seemed meaner and scarier. I was not comfortable breaking laws, and I hated and feared violence. I have never been able to call anyone a "pig." America in 1969 was a polarized country, much as it is today, and I didn't like living in a country divided. So I hitchhiked to Mexico for the summer, and then worked in Europe for a year.

When I returned to Nebraska, I began a Ph.D. program in psychology, married Jim, and, for the next twenty years, was a mom and a therapist. While my children were growing up, I attended ball games, swim meets, recitals, and school spaghetti dinners. We all piled into our VW bus and went on camping vacations. In my free time, such as it was, I read. My actions for the greater good consisted of small donations of money, and even smaller donations of time.

Adults are most alike when raising children. Whether we are Democrats or Republicans, adventurous or cautious, brilliant or dull, Unitarians, Jews, or Evangelical Christians, we do pretty much the same things during the child-rearing years. We change diapers, do laundry, read stories aloud, buy groceries, make chicken soup and brownies, and attend child-focused events. Before we were parents, we did many things that are uniquely our own, and, later, when the kids leave, we will do our own thing again. For the time being, children's needs dictate our activities.

As my children grew, I became more involved in local politics. I served on the Human Rights commission. My daughter and I worked at a homeless shelter, and washed dishes at a soup kitchen. These activities were worthy, but they didn't answer my central question: What needs doing that only I can do?

Then, in the late 1980s, for the first time since I was a girl I had a little discretionary time. I had the luxury of asking myself, What do I want to do with my extra hours? My answer roared out from deep within me: I want to write. I have always wanted to write. I do not care if I am no good at it. I just want to try.

My expectations were low. I had written my first poem when I was twelve, a sonnet, and turned it in to my teacher. She handed it back with a big C marked at the top, and the comment "Trite." It was about this same time that I had confessed to my father that I wanted to be a writer, and he had responded, "No one makes any money at that. Be a doctor like your mom so that you can take care of yourself."

I saw the world at that time as divided into brilliant, interesting people with great gifts and common people like me with great aspirations but no gifts. As a girl from a small Nebraska town, I felt that my life would be of absolutely no interest to others. Action and drama happened someplace far away, in the cities visited by the trains that roared by in the middle of the night. I gave up on myself then. I loved writing too much to do it badly.

But then, at age forty-three, I dove in. I signed up for a course at the local university. My teacher was a football coach from Texas who liked horse races, bowling, and liquor, but he could teach. He regaled us with stories of writers he had known, told jokes, and tossed off tips. He said, "Never use 'needless to say' as a phrase. If it is needless to say, don't say it." And, "If your message is life is shit, spare the reader." He also told us not to have our characters "begin to" do anything. "Just let them get down to business right away," he said.

Mostly, he encouraged us. He emphasized that writing was difficult, but not impossible, to learn. After he read my first story, he said, "You could be a writer," and when I left his office I wept. That day was my christening. Like almost all writers, I had been waiting a long time to hear those words. Until we receive some kind of external validation of our writing, some of us find it hard to believe in ourselves.

At first, I did not connect my writing to social activism. Soon, however, I relished writing letters to editors, op-ed pieces, book reviews, and commentaries for Nebraska Public Radio. Around this time (1989), my therapy practice was suddenly swamped with women who were losing control of their eating. They were bingeing and purging, starving or food-obsessed, and unable to eat normally. Some were merely bemoaning fat thighs or double chins; others were being admitted to hospitals with arrhythmias or punctured esophagi. My friends and my daughter's friends also were worried about their bodies. Meanwhile, then as now, magazines pushed contradictory messages at women: "Be thin" . . . "Bake these double chocolate brownies."

Seeing all the needless pain, I decided to write a *j'accuse* kind of book about women and weight. I wanted to examine cultural messages, not the psyches of individual women. And I wanted to have an impact. As I wrote *Hunger Pains,* the great strands of my life wove together for the first time. My love of books and of writing twined around my work as a therapist and my yearning to make the world a better place. I felt scared and inadequate, but I was ready to give it a go.

As you write a history of yourself, you will notice many things. Perhaps one of your parents died of lung cancer, and you want to write op-ed pieces calling for smoking bans. Or your grandparents were refugees, and you want to write to help newcomers. Or perhaps a teacher instilled in you a love of art museums, and you wish to promote children's art programs.

Wonderful or terrible events can inspire activism. Great injustice may create an Eldridge Cleaver, a Martin Luther King, or a Harriet Beecher Stowe. But joy and awe also create activists. Many people discover their missions while pondering a sky filled with stars or walking through the forest. Think Edward Abbey. Think John Muir.

Growing our souls could be defined as the steady accretion of empathy, clarity, and passion for the good. It is an increase in our sense of who we call "us," as well as an expansion in our capacity to draw distinctions and make connections. Our lives are journeys toward a certain kind of wisdom, which is a love and appreciation for all living creatures. All animals, carefully observed, have things to teach us. And so does every person we encounter. Zulus sum up the need for human connection this way: "A person is a person through other persons." We grow wise in the context of our culture. And we can define our culture as the sum total of our interactions with people and animals and the land. Skilled writers are able to somehow make that interaction into conversation, even making it more inclusive and richer than originally.

Research psychologists have found that there are two distinct kinds of moral courage, and that one does not predicate the other. People can lead heroic lives due to their character. Hannah Arendt, Eleanor Roosevelt, Joanna Macy, and Arundhati Roy come to mind. Or people can have greatness thrust upon them by accident. For example, a man who has never been particularly heroic may rush into a burning building to save its residents. A moral awakening can be triggered by a specific event, as with the case of Samantha Power, author of *A Problem from Hell: America and the Age of Genocide*. Power was a sports fan whose goal was to be the female Bob Costas. However, one night, while she working a Braves game in Atlanta, the news of Tiananmen Square came across the wire. Power was so moved by that tragedy that she decided that her life was meant for a different purpose. She is now a leading expert on and advocate for human rights and the prevention of mass violence.

I urge you to write your own stories, to tell us what in your history made you the person you are today. The deeper you explore your own life, the more ways you will discover to connect yourself to the great and universal human stories.

The following chapter presents a recent example of my activist writing. During the summer of 2004, I was alarmed and depressed about the state of the world. I wrote the piece to change the conversation in our country. My friend Rich Simon published it in *Psychotherapy Networker*. More than almost anything I have written, it weaves together the important strands of my life: psychology, writing, and social commentary.

FIVE

MR. USA

Assessment Report on Mr. USA

Client name: Mr. United States of America

Address: Western Hemisphere, North of the Equator, Planet Earth

Description of client: Mr. USA was born July 4, 1776, and was 228 years old at the time of this assessment. He appeared as a well-dressed, rather heavy, middle-aged man with a somewhat arrogant manner. Still, he had moments when he was charming, humorous, and appealingly open. During our interview, Mr. USA looked anxious and exhausted. He was forgetful and had difficulty concentrating. When a car alarm sounded, he exhibited a strong startle response. Parenthetically, a squirrel had inadvertently triggered the antitheft device on Mr. USA's oversized Sports Utility Vehicle.

Presenting problem: Mr. USA made this appointment two years after an assault on September 11, 2001, that caused him great physical harm and mental anguish. This tragedy reopened scars from earlier traumas in his life, such as Pearl Harbor, Vietnam, and the bombing in Oklahoma City. A series of bad decisions, including adopting the Patriot Act, a preemptive attack on Iraq, and violation of the Geneva

Conventions, has forced him to confront his mental health issues. As this client's life has spiraled out of control, his colleagues at the United Nations have encouraged him to seek therapy.

As we talked, it became clear that even before 9/11, Mr. USA had not been dealing with his problems in a healthy fashion. For the last forty years, he's grown increasingly overwhelmed and lonely. While his fortunes have fluctuated during this period, his overall quality of life has steadily diminished. Especially during these last few decades, he has lost the capacity to simply relax and have fun. Mr. USA suffers from multiple addictions: caffeine, sugar, alcohol, drugs, nicotine, shopping, gambling, watching television, and playing video games. His finances are a mess.

History: Mr. USA reports a violent birth and a turbulent difficult life. Yet he acknowledges many happy, peaceful times. He comes from a family that values education, art, and music. However, he lacks discipline and, given his opportunities, is not as well educated as he might be. He's been exposed to many religious belief systems: Catholic, Buddhist, Jewish, Protestant, and Muslim. Currently, he is an Evangelical Christian, although in religion, as in many other aspects of his life, Mr. USA is in conflict with himself.

During the early decades of his life, Mr. USA found himself frequently in fights, but he was never seriously injured. When he was in his eighties, he was in a violent altercation that he refers to as the Civil War. Scars from that event still fester. Roughly seventy years ago, he suffered a decade of dust storms, bank failures, high unemployment, and severe poverty. Because he thought clearly and acted decisively, he pulled through that period with admirable resilience. He has fought several other brawls in the last one hundred years, some started by him, some by others.

Mr. USA values independence over connection, and freedom over obligations and commitments. He boasts of his Declaration of Independence and War of Independence, and he calls his birthday Independence Day. He crafted a Bill of Rights, but no corresponding Bill of Responsibilities. He is a doer not a thinker, and fares better with men than with women. He has trouble sharing, compromising, and keeping his promises. His bullying and tantrums have soured numerous relationships. He has an unreasonable, perhaps delusional, view of how he is perceived. He likes to see himself as altruistic, but many of his choices have harmed his fellow nations.

Mr. USA's oldest friendships are with countries in Western Europe; however, currently, he is not close to any of those friends, except England. He reports that even England doesn't seem to want to spend much time with him. This social isolation could be detrimental to Mr. USA's mental health.

Mr. USA suffers from the effects of his addictions. He has poor vision, hypertension, and a sluggish metabolism. He's restless and moody. While he tests in the superior range intellectually, he is not functioning at that level. His mental impairments appear to be stress related, and could be reversed with therapy and healthier lifestyle choices.

Personality features: Even though chronologically an adult, Mr. USA has regressed to functioning as a social and emotional adolescent. His ideas are extreme, shallow, and rigidly held. He indulges in either/or and us/them thinking. He demonizes his enemies without making any effort to understand them. He lacks basic factual knowledge, and has trouble with perspective. He considers himself exceptional, and has great difficulty understanding others' points of view.

Mr. USA appears incapable of long-term planning. He acts on

the basis of short-term desires, and exhibits low frustration tolerance. He values style over substance, and is preoccupied with sex. Like most aggressive individuals, he overuses violence as a solution, and minimizes and/or justifies antisocial behavior.

As is common with traumatized clients, Mr. USA has regressed in terms of his moral development. He is hunkered down and defensive, always worrying about himself. He is greedy in a world of people in desperate need of basic resources. Mr. USA insists that his fellow nations obey rules that he violates at will. This behavior is particularly irritating to others because, based on his past history, they expect better of him.

He believes in buy now, pay later, and frequently makes poor choices about time, money, and relationships. He spends lavishly on weapons systems and baubles, but neglects to budget for his own health, education, and home maintenance. He flees from pain, and avoids, rather than deals with, his problems. His main attitude seems to be, If I ignore it, maybe it will go away. He's adopted this attitude with the AIDS epidemic, global warming, the population explosion, and economic and social injustice.

Under a flimsy veneer of bravado, Mr. USA is shell-shocked by a world that is too complex emotionally and cognitively for him to understand. What appears as frenetic activity is disguised despair. He's awash in contradictions and paralyzed by indecision. He lacks mental clarity and focus, as exemplified by his attention to inconsequential issues such as whether Janet Jackson intended to show her breast at a Super Bowl event.

Mr. USA experiences daily panic attacks. While some of his fears, such as those concerning terrorism, SARS, or the world's fifty thousand atomic bombs, are realistic, others are self-induced and even paranoid. His media, his advertisers, and his politicians keep him hypervigilant. Of course, many of his fears are both realistic *and* exaggerated. As we psychologists say, Just because you're paranoid doesn't mean they aren't out to get you.

Character structure: Mr. USA is a decent man. He likes to be called Uncle Sam, and there have been times in his history when he merited that fine moniker. He has assisted his neighbors in floods and famines, and, after World War II, he helped reconstruct Europe. Since 9/11, he has been more self-absorbed and immature than usual. However, he is not a psychopath or career criminal. He wants to be loved, and to behave properly. Historically, he's served as a model for the world in terms of freedom, cultural development, and opportunity for all. If he can control his anxiety and his temper, his friends will eagerly return to his life.

Diagnosis: Post-traumatic stress disorder, multiple addictions. Rule out delusions.

Personal strengths: Mr. USA has great natural talent, wealth, and potentially good looks if he lost some weight. He is a mixture of almost all the peoples of the world: Latino, Native American, Asian, African, Middle Eastern, and European. His family life is rich in traditions from every corner of our planet. He has many support systems in place—county fairs, bluegrass festivals, public libraries, and a host of restorative retreats he calls national parks. He contains within himself Annie Oakley, Stephen Foster, Sacajawea, Louisa May Alcott, Thomas Jefferson, Ralph Stanley, Edward Hopper, W. C. Fields, Lance Armstrong, Henry Moore, Martin Luther King Jr., Stanley Kunitz, Humphrey Bogart, Abe Lincoln, Venus and Serena Williams, Crazy Horse, Mark Twain, Louis Armstrong, Cesar Chávez, and Ethel Waters. He's resourceful, resilient, and pragmatic. And even though it wasn't apparent at the time of our interview, he's been sensible and peace loving during much of his life. Even in his worst times, Mr. USA has been capable of heroic acts, kindness, and creative problem solving.

Treatment plan: Mr. USA must begin by telling the truth. He needs to accept his mistakes, blind spots, and dark side, including his history of genocide of Native Americans, slavery with African Americans, and his mistreatment of immigrants. He must acknowledge his sabotaging of democracies in Africa and Latin America, and the blood on his hands from his governmental and trade policies.

As a victim of post-traumatic stress disorder, Mr. USA must work through various stages of grief: shock and denial, sorrow, anger, resolution, and moving on with hope. He could greatly benefit from lessons in impulse control and stoicism. Self-awareness is not Mr. USA's strong suit, but he must grow in this area if he is to survive and help the world community endure.

He needs detoxification from too much television and advertising, and needs to reconnect to his own past and world history. Mr. USA requires clear, honest feedback about the effects of his behavior on others. Currently, he has limited access to important indices that concern the quality of his life. He doesn't know what is in his air, food, or water, or how many of his resources are disappearing daily. He attends tangential measurements, such as the Dow Jones and the gross domestic product, and misses the big picture.

His therapist will be most helpful if she helps him establish an identity not connected to sports, competition, or war. Rather, treatment requires metaphors of hope, reconciliation, and cooperation. He needs to feel that his actions matter, that he can achieve success if he works hard, and that he is not alone.

Mr. USA will feel better when he realizes that there is no "us" and no "them." There is a great world heart that beats, and like Eritrea, France, Iran, and New Zealand, he inhabits the body fed by that mother heart.

Progress milestones: As this client improves, he will be less violent, and less obsessed with sex, shopping, and drugs. The tensions between his different parts will subside, and he'll benefit from a less compartmentalized, more integrated personality structure. He'll be calmer, and more honest and authentic.

Mr. USA will participate in more potluck dinners and fewer hostile takeovers. His streets will be full of people walking and talking to one another. People of all races and ethnic groups will share the best of their cultures with one another. His children will beg to go to school where, in addition to learning science, geography, math, literature, and history, they sing, act, dance, write poetry, and become skilled in emotional intelligence. His old people will be treated with great love and respect. Mr. USA will join with other nations to build a clean, healthy, and fair world. A Department of Peace will be established and funded. Nations all over the world will once again befriend and respect Mr. USA.

Prognosis: A good therapist will help this client to appreciate and develop all of his talents, and foster a world community where others also may flourish. Mr. USA is in crisis, which may motivate him to grow in new directions. He has the opportunity to emerge from this trauma a wiser and deeper person.

Respectfully submitted, Dr. Mary Pipher

PART TWO

The Writing Process

SIX

DIVING IN—GETTING STARTED

To make an apple pie from scratch, you must first invent the
universe. —CARL SAGAN

Write a little every day, without hope, without despair.
—ISAK DINESEN

Three times a week, I go to the university recreation center to
swim. The water temperature hovers around sixty-eight degrees,
and in the winter, especially after I have walked across the icy cam-
pus, it requires courage to dive in. I shiver by the edge of the water,
my legs knobby with goose bumps. I invent reasons not to go swimming—I have a slight sore throat, or I might be late for a meeting—
then I dive in. I do not stick my toe in or I might chicken out. I just
dive. As I swim as fast as I can to warm up, I gasp for breath. The
first few laps are punishing, but then it becomes easier. My muscles
warm up, and the water seems friendlier. My thinking is energized
and my body is awake. I lose track of time. When I am finished, I am
sorry I can't swim longer.

A blank page can feel like cold water. We can be afraid of what will happen next. We can come up with good reasons to delay. We can make excuses and psych ourselves out. Yet we can't let ourselves turn away—we have to dive in. And when we do, it can be miserable until we warm up. Then we relax and write without effort. We are in flow.

> The secret of getting ahead is getting started.
> —AGATHA CHRISTIE
>
> A good writer always works at the impossible.
> —JOHN STEINBECK
>
> What I had that others didn't was a capacity for sticking to it.
> —DORIS LESSING
>
> A writer is someone for whom writing is more difficult than for others.
> —THOMAS MANN

Our biggest plunge is taking ourselves seriously. Many of us find it difficult to simply state, "I am a writer." We fumble and mumble around—"I'm not really a writer," or "I don't consider myself a real writer, but . . ." When we equivocate, we lose an opportunity to build our identities as writers. If you are not saying it already, I advise you to learn to say you are a writer.

All writers share a deep desire to communicate, but our skills and temperaments are not givens. Some writers can toss off pearls at whim; most of us, however, are trudgers. We learn to put our behinds in the chair and stay there. Writing, like every other complex craft, takes most of us years to master. In that apprenticeship period, many of us experience a great deal of frustration, rejection, and failure. Indeed, one thing that successful writers share is their ability to tolerate defeat and soldier on.

We learn to take our projects one day at a time: "Inch by inch, it's a cinch. Yard by yard, it's hard." We give ourselves permission to write lousy first drafts. For most writers, it is much easier to improve writing than to get it right the first time. When the poet William Stafford was asked how he was able to write a poem every day, he responded, "I lower my standards."

> Work inspires inspiration. Keep working. If you succeed, keep working. If you fail, keep working. If you are interested, keep working. If you are bored, keep working.
>
> —MICHAEL CRICHTON

Some people have the temperament to be writers but lack the talent. In my opinion, many more people have the talent than the temperament. The talent is basically observational skills and verbal facility. The ideal writer's temperament includes the ability to tolerate ambiguity, handle intensity, wrestle with self-doubt, take risks, and accurately assess criticism. Most writers must be able to withstand poverty, loneliness, and anguish. And we also must be able to motivate ourselves to keep going in the face of the world's total indifference.

Writers tend to be sensitive people, and yet to write we need to be tough. Change writers in particular require a certain stolidity to deal with adversity. Editorial writer Ellen Goodman exhibits such toughness when dealing with hate mail: "I give very few people the right to make me feel badly." When we write about important issues, we will inevitably be challenged. Others will feel equally passionately about these issues, but from the opposite points of view. To manage the intense reactions of others, we "need to put the footsteps of courage into the stirrups of patience," as explorer and writer Ernest Shackleton put it.

We are interested in our own thought processes. Skilled writers pay attention when the muse or any other internal visitor comes to call. Poet Marjorie Saiser describes the muse as a "polite little girl." She will come up when we are busy and tug at our shirt. If we ignore her, she will go away. If we want her in our work, we must be ready to attend her gentle call.

In fact, to write well we must be in touch with our emotions. When we sit down to write, we may not be feeling anything much. But as we write, we want to connect with our submerged feelings. Many poets read poetry to open their hearts to the writing process. Nonfiction writer Melissa Fay Greene listens to classical music. Still others meditate or watch the landscape so that they can dive deep into their feelings and thoughts before they begin working.

> If a writer stops observing he is finished. Experience is communicated by small details intimately observed.
>
> —ERNEST HEMINGWAY

Writers walk many roads, but we share certain crossroads. One such crossroad is observation. Writers are curious people who imbibe the world. Most of us eavesdrop on other people's conversations, read voraciously, and even note what others are reading on subways or at the grocery store.

Writers pay attention to both the external and internal landscapes. We note the look a wife gives her husband when he asks her to pick up the check at a café, or the way a child runs to meet her grandmother at the airport baggage claim. We notice a man riding a bicycle in winter, or that our hotel room maid looks stressed, or the child in our apartment building who never seems to smile.

For me, what most represents this yearning to pay attention to the world is a photograph of the Spanish playwright and poet Federico García Lorca, taken shortly before he was killed in the Spanish Civil War. Staring fiercely at the camera, Lorca looks young and heartbreakingly intense, with his shiny black hair and haunted eyes. Under his image, he has scribbled, *"Presente, presente, presente"* (I am here, I am here, I am here).

Be Bold. Be Honest

Many of us must unlearn how to write badly. Perhaps in school our writing was evaluated by the number of pages produced. Or in college we learned to write cautiously, always citing others' ideas instead of our own. Maybe we were warned away from being subjective. Unless we were fortunate enough to always have had great teachers, we have learned some lessons that will not serve us well.

Until I was in my late thirties, I approached writing with the blandness and caution endemic to many academics. I "caveated" everything. I was afraid to assert myself or think beyond the conventional body of wisdom. My conclusions were decaffeinated with skim, so small as to be in the Who cares anyway? category.

I sorted out my major writing mistakes when I wrote *Reviving Ophelia*. Yawning while reading my timid first drafts was a sobering experience. I resolved not to hold back. I slashed and burned through my manuscript, crossing out every "Based on the previous information, we could tentatively conclude for certain populations . . ." and instead wrote "We live in a girl-poisoning culture," and "Young girls experience a Bermuda Triangle of dangers in early adolescence, and many go down with the storm."

The first effect of this change in tone was that it enlivened me. I started having fun, and being truly excited by what I was writing. And as I cut my writing style loose, my thinking roamed more freely. Happily, I realized I was inventing new ideas.

I tried to delete obvious statements and conventional wisdom. When I wrote exactly what I had expected to write, I bored myself. I discovered that one path into original thinking was to ask myself, Okay, that is your first idea. What are your second and third ideas? At the end of the day, I would reexamine my work, and think, Can I honestly argue something even more daring and unique?

For writers, surprises flag the original and the personal. Recently, I read Kimberly French's article "Bitter Harvest" in the *Unitarian Universalist World*. She dives into the story with this surprising opening: "You, in all likelihood, own items produced by slaves. Chocolate. Handwoven carpets. Coffee. Tea. Tobacco. Sugar. Tomatoes. Cucumbers. Oranges . . ." Sharing her own amazement at discovering that slavery exists today all over the world, including in the United States, French ends her piece with questions for her readers: "What good is our economic and political power if we can't use it to free slaves? If we can't choose to stop slavery, how can we say we are free?" Not pallid prose.

Wrestling Demons

Feelings of inadequacy are the black lung disease of writing.
—CHARLES BAXTER

It's hell writing, but it's hell not writing. The only tolerable state is just having written. —ROBERT HASS

The human race is a race of cowards. I am not only marching in the parade, I am carrying a banner. —MARK TWAIN

Demons are internal pressures such as exhaustion, illness, debilitating sorrow, mental health problems, or addictions. I can't name all possible demons, let alone explore them fully. Some demons are angry or craving, others are slothful or envious. Some are profligate, others despairing and filled with self-doubt.

I am not fond of the phrase "writer's block." It is an overused, fuzzy term that sometimes simply describes laziness and apathy. Generally, we can deconstruct writer's block systematically by exploring our own personal issues. We all have our demons, but we are not beyond salvation. The trick is facing them, not running from them, and directing them toward a purpose. If we can endure them without panic or despair, they will weaken and we grow stronger, and not just at writing.

Anxiety was my personal demon. I can be a real worrier and self-flagellator. I never experienced writer's block in terms of not being able to think of anything to write about. My fear caused me to write such mealymouthed prose that, at the end of the day, I was tempted to delete everything. My despair about my bad writing was reinforced by the fact that I was a good reader. I truly knew I was writing badly.

I had so much respect for writing that I was cowed by the thought of joining the community of writers. One way I fended off anxiety was to keep track of the number of hours I wrote each day. I told myself that I had a certain number of IQ points and a certain personality. Those were givens that I could not change. But I could work hard. I kept track of my hours just so I could tell myself, Calm down. You have put in your time.

Always I prepared for the next day's writing by stopping at a moment when I felt exhilarated by a good sentence or paragraph. That allowed me to have a slightly happy feeling when I left my study, and less dread when I came back the next morning. I wasn't starting out stuck; I was jumping back into flow.

Still, like many writers, every morning I resisted approaching my writing work. When I woke, I was tempted to read the paper, unload the dishwasher, or watch the birds at the feeder. I tricked myself into working by saying to myself, Mary, you can have a cup of coffee at your desk. I dawdled in the kitchen, but soon I wanted caffeine, so I poured a big cup and meandered into the study.

I wrote in my journal. It was nonthreatening, and it woke me up. I read from my collection of books on writing. Then I tackled business letters, thank-you notes, and cards to friends. Again, the easy stuff. By that time, I had been working for an hour and was ready to turn to more serious endeavors.

I tried to keep a range of projects on my desk. Sometimes I chose by topic, but more often than not I selected tasks according to my mental acumen, which waxed and waned. On slow days, I edited, read over past work, constructed an outline, or did research. On better days, I did free writes, or continued work on a chapter or essay. On halcyon days, I thought through the thorniest problems: What is the central core of my argument? What is shallow and trivial? What contradictions does my piece contain? What am I missing?

Some days, until I dealt with my internal critic I was too anxious to work. I would embrace her, and tell her to calm down and enjoy life. I wrote out all her nasty criticisms until I was amused or exhausted. Paradoxically, allowing the critic to speak quieted her down. I could laugh at how ridiculous she sounded when I gave her a voice. However, I would never speak to another writer that way.

The writer Craig Vetter once remarked, "The Brooklyn Bridge was built by a guy who had a term paper to write." When Vetter lectured at Nebraska Wesleyan University, he told an amusing story about his unfinished "great American novel." He said he kept it on his desk at all times. He woke every morning so daunted by the prospect of touching it that he always turned to an easier project. He said, "I've written several books while waiting to write that novel."

Paradoxically, even though writing is anxiety provoking, it is also therapeutic. Once we are immersed in writing, we forget our anxiety. Focusing on clarity and beauty calms us down. I think back to my friends, myself, and people all over the world writing after 9/11. We wrote out our sorrow, our terror, our anger, and our struggles to make sense of events. Stewing in our own stress is not a good way to handle difficulty. Action ameliorates anxiety.

Support

My writing group is called the "Prairie Trout." We named ourselves by choosing two beautiful nouns and slamming them together, often a good way to name a group, a band, or a book. We five women have shared our writing since 1992. With one exception, we are all small-town Nebraska women. We are all mothers, gardeners, bird-watchers, and readers who lead simple lives organized around family and friends.

We all write in many genres. We meet once a month and read our work aloud. We listen to the reader and ask questions, or tell the reader what we heard or understood. Sometimes, we offer specific advice about content, plot, word choice, grammar, or tone. We may recommend changing emphasis or point of view. We often praise, but we also share our confusion, or our sense that a piece needs more development.

There are no rules, really, except to be kind and brave. We try to allocate the time fairly. We bring each other news of readings, contests, workshops, retreats, and residencies. Some of the Trout meet at cafés to write together. Collectively, we teach, give readings, and appear on panels.

We have helped each other grow. We have corrected mistakes gently, and cheered each other on. We have soothed and joked with each other when we received rejections, and we have celebrated one another's victories. In short, we have built our writing lives together.

The Trout are responsible for *Reviving Ophelia*'s success. When I took my proposal to them, they were interested in the topic. I told them I planned to name my book *The Social, Emotional, and Cognitive Issues of Early Adolescent Females.* The Trout howled with laughter. They all agreed they would never buy a book with that title. They urged me to consider something metaphorical, maybe from Shakespeare—always a classy choice.

My town has dozens of groups, some public and others private. But if you can't find a group, start one. Two people can constitute a writer's group. Ask a friend to join you, or post a notice in your church bulletin, at the local bookstore, or in the teacher's lounge at school. Most groups have a few rules: Just read your work. Don't apologize or explain. Let the writing stand alone. Share the time fairly. Support the work of others whenever you can. Keep what is read and said in the group confidential. Some groups require new work every meeting, which often helps writers keep producing. Necessity sharpens focus. In a productive group, members respect one another's work, and they have discovered the knack of providing direct feedback that is also optimistic and kind. Foremost, they trust one another to tell the truth.

Some writers proceed without formal groups, but often they have an informal group of encouragers. When you join a writers' group, you become part of a community that appreciates how difficult it is to write well and how much it hurts to receive rejections. We writers do such arduous and sometimes discouraging work that almost all of us can benefit from the support and feedback of others. I urge you to find a home in a community of people who will become your writing family.

Time

> The problems in life are to a great degree the problems of attention.   —CHARLES JOHNSON
>
> We can spend our whole lives fishing only to discover in the end it wasn't fish we were after.   —THOREAU
>
> The barn is burned down now, I can see the moon.
>
> —MASAHIDE

In our lifetimes, we can do many things, but not everything. Especially as we age, what Allen Ginsberg called the "alphabet soup of time" becomes an increasingly important factor in our decision making. As one friend put it, "Time is the real money now."

Just like everyone else, writers experience sorrows and stressors—bills to pay, needy friends, health needs, and sick relatives, plus all the sad little details of ordinary life. Of course, joys also can keep us from our work—sunrises, children, ball games, parties, concerts, and vacations. All of these things interrupt our attention yet simultaneously give us something to write about.

It seems ironic that often those who are most curious and engaged with the world have the least time to think about it and share their thoughts. Wise activists know that part of changing the world involves periodically cloistering oneself from it. Charles Dickens walked an hour for every hour he wrote. The Dalai Lama rises at 3

A.M. to meditate for several hours before beginning his busy day. Many environmental activists retreat to beautiful places to rest and refuel before reentering the fray.

Both writing and meditating are ways to expand and enrich time. In meditation, we learn to examine our thoughts and feelings from a new perspective, to watch the river of our consciousness flow by, observing it but not attaching ourselves to it. We train ourselves to have a meta-consciousness that observes ourselves observing, and that enlarges moments into infinity. In writing, we also develop that meta-consciousness. We experience our lives as lived events, but also as material to be carefully examined later for richness and meaning. Just as meditation makes life more aware and joyous, so writing allows us to live more deeply and fully. Both involve the sanctification of time.

SEVEN

THE PSYCHOLOGY OF CHANGE

The real voyage of discovery is not in seeking new places, but in seeing with new eyes. ——MARCEL PROUST

The purpose of life is to be happy and to make others happy. ——THE DALAI LAMA

A book ought to be an ax to break the frozen sea within us. ——ANTON CHEKHOV

Psychotherapy might be called the science and art of establishing relationships. It allows people who do not know each other, and who come from profoundly different backgrounds, worldviews, and circumstances, to engage in honest conversations that often lead to personal transformation. This transformation happens because therapy has rules of engagement, developed over decades, and based on premises such as that the way people enter into a conversation influences its outcome and that true change occurs only in the context of relationships.

Therapy and writing have a great deal in common. Both are highly disciplined endeavors, involving long hours in small rooms. Both require asking intelligent questions, excavating for emotional truths, and solving complex problems. Often, the work is ambiguous, and success elusive. Wise therapists help clients to think more clearly, feel more deeply, and behave more responsibly. Wise writers often want to do these same things.

Both writers and therapists develop professional voices and styles. Both build up these skills by using who they are and what they know. Therapists find themselves attracted to certain personality theories and therapy styles. Depending on their talents, interests, and skills, they cobble together a way of interacting that is effective. Writers also develop a sense of what works best for them.

Writers and therapists connect with others when they speak or write in an accessible language. Intelligence is a virtue in both professions, but it should not call attention to itself. As Isaac Asimov noted, "I gave up on being brilliant when I was eighteen. I am perfectly willing to let the reader take it for granted I know all the long words. I don't have to constantly demonstrate it."

In general, both therapists and change agents must train themselves to stay attentive, calm, and kind. We must strive to keep anxiety or anger from interfering with our work. With our presence and attention, we suggest that honest exploration of issues is healing and that hiding from them is toxic. These are simple but not easy things to do. Philosopher Benjamin Ward writes of linguistic determinism that naming determines action and that which is unnamed is ignored. By naming in therapy or writing, we expand clients' or readers' consciousness.

As the poet Adrienne Rich said, "That which is unspoken becomes unspeakable." By our writing, we suggest that no topic is so overwhelming or horrid that it cannot be discussed honestly. Sex abuse, gay bashing, torture, or slavery can be subjects for analysis. In *Man's Search for Meaning*, Viktor Frankl tackled the Holocaust in a way that helped millions of people learn lessons from this almost unimaginable event.

Rules of Engagement
for Change Agents

> I shall allow no man to belittle my soul by making me hate
> him. —BOOKER T. WASHINGTON

RESPECT

Therapists can succeed only with people whom they respect, which is not as difficult as it sounds. Most people are sympathetic when we hear their stories from their point of view. Clients do not have to be likable or even reasonable for therapists to respect them. They just need to be trying to improve.

Contempt shows, and it always becomes mutual. It evokes defensiveness and fear, which poison the change process. Attacks cause all of us to build the walls around ourselves even higher. Respect helps us relax around each other enough to contemplate changing.

Martin Luther King Jr. underscored the importance of respect in his essay "The Call of Service." He encouraged civil rights workers not to stereotype or label their adversaries as rednecks, crackers, or fools. He argued that all people are multifaceted, and that to divide the world into us and them was to risk joining the ranks of the opponents.

ACCURATE EMPATHY

We have to look deeply at things in order to see. When a swimmer enjoys the clear water of the river, he or she should also be able to be the river.   —THICH NHAT HANH

A great deal of the work of both writers and therapists could be called empathy training. We help people sample one another's fates. Therapists ask, How do you think Y felt when you said X? Change writers ask the same type of questions. For example, in *True Notebooks* Mark Saltzman describes his experience teaching creative writing at Central Juvenile Hall, a lockup for Los Angeles's most violent teenage offenders. He allows stories from the classroom and his students' writing to speak to his readers. And he doesn't editorialize. As I read, I stopped judging and stereotyping those I had previously labeled as "gang members." I was profoundly moved by Saltzman's descriptions of real people struggling to make sense of their lives. For the duration of the book, and then beyond, I could see the world from their points of view.

However, there is a profound difference between therapy and writing. Therapists are physically present with their clients. They look them in the eye, and watch their facial and body movements and their breathing. And clients scrutinize their therapists too. They are entrained. Writers, on the other hand, do not face their readers directly. Instead, we focus on the page and confront our own ideas. We are immersed in a process that is inner-directed. In his book *The Reader Over Your Shoulder,* Robert Graves advises writers to immerse themselves in the creative process but to save a small amount of attention for readers. Excellent advice. Thinking too much about readers makes writers self-conscious. Writers want a free flow of unedited ideas; but, occasionally, we need to glance over our shoulders.

Poet laureate Ted Kooser said the same thing using a different metaphor. He wrote, "If you keep the shadow of that reader—like a whiff of perfume—in the room where you write, you will be a better writer."

Therapists influence one person at a time, while writers hope to reach as many readers as possible with our words. Yet, in reality, we too influence one person at a time. Every reader has his or her own reactions to our ideas. Readers know us sometimes better than our nonreader friends, and they interact with our ideas, feelings, aesthetics, and sensibilities on every page. We are in a relationship.

The therapist Carl Rogers was the wisest of change agents. He did not suggest "Be like me," or "Do this," or "Improve yourself." He communicated, "I accept you totally." When he conveyed that message, his clients began to transform themselves.

Think of change agents as tour guides. With competent, pleasant guides, people will travel almost anywhere. With an untrustworthy, surly guide, they won't even take a cab across town for dinner at the Four Seasons.

CONNECTION

If the three secrets of successful restaurants are location, location, location, the three secrets of persuasion are connection, connection, connection. As writers, we do best when we assume that our readers are good-hearted and energetic, as well as, busy, anxious, and confused. We can also safely assume that readers are unlikely to be fully aware of our favorite issues. As news commentator Eric Sevareid said, "Never underestimate the reader's intelligence or overestimate his information level." We have things to teach readers, but we must be careful doing it. They will resent us if we make them feel manipulated or stupid.

Race, politics, and cultural background prompt various reactions to words such as "police," "border patrol," and "affirmative action." "Emotional" tends to mean different things to men and women. Women associate the word with warmth, caring, and openness, while men associate it with hysteria and being out of control. "Apologize" is a relatively straightforward and uncomplicated word to most women that means "I am sorry that you feel badly," or "I made a mistake. I am sorry if it hurt you in any way." To many men, "apologize" is a dreadful word that means "I have to humble myself and beg forgiveness."

CLARITY

Change agents need to make clear distinctions. For example, newscaster Daniel Schorr, in speaking about the Bush foreign policy under Condoleezza Rice, said, "It will be more cohesive, if not more coherent." By this comment he meant that our government's foreign policies would be more integrated and uniform, but not necessarily more rational or functional. This nuanced use of words is evidence of a clear thinker.

Recently, a hunter wrote my local paper in response to a story about men "hunting" on the Internet. These men paid several hundred dollars for the privilege of shooting, from the comfort of their own homes, a deer or a bear on a faraway Texas ranch. They could view these animals on their computer screen and then kill them by manipulating their mouse to point and shoot a gun. To the man who wrote into our paper, these men were not hunters; to him, hunting meant partaking in an ancient ritual that involved being in a relationship with land and animals. He argued that people who entered that sacred relationship were hunters, while people who did not were merely animal killers. This distinction is another example of clarity.

PERSPECTIVE

One of my rules as a therapist was: Don't let the urgent crowd out the important. Certain clients had a crisis every week, and we could have spent all our time sorting these out. But I felt the need to go deeper, to say, "Let's put this in the context of the larger patterns of your life."

Writers too can guide readers toward the important rather than the urgent. Daily headlines scream out stories of celebrity divorces, horrendous crimes, or gruesome deaths—tragic stories for the individuals involved, but ultimately perhaps not as important as the melting of the polar ice caps or the equitable and sustainable distribution of resources among all peoples. Quiet catastrophes, without good visuals, tend to be overlooked. In our great postmodern supermarket of ideas, good writers point readers toward meaning.

As connectors, we want to avoid dichotomies. Black-and-white thinking in others is unlikely to be changed if we employ the same thinking ourselves. Either/or thinking is simply not nuanced enough to reflect reality. Business success and economic justice need not be opposites. Women's rights are not antifamily. Both/and thinking connects everything, and leaves room for new ideas as well. We do not want to become what we fear most: fanatics. (Churchill once defined fanatics as people who won't change their minds and can't change the subject.)

We want to offer readers the courage of our doubts as well as our convictions. On paper, we can explore our own unresolved issues and unanswered questions. Everything does not have to be presented to readers as an open-and-shut case.

"Complex" is a respectful word to use in therapy with feuding couples. It implies, We need time to work. There are things happening here that we don't understand. It also implies that there are different, yet equally valid, points of view on the subject. To use this word is to suggest that the truth is rarely pure and never simple.

Change agents frame experience for readers or clients. Any frame intensifies what is inside it. A frame selects a small drop of water from the river of reality and says, Let us examine this for the essence of our situation. Creative work involves choosing frames that enlighten and inspire. With a client, I might say, "Let us discuss the way you greeted me when you came in today. That may teach us something about our relationship." As writers, we select tiny slices of the universe that we use to reflect much larger pieces. For example, I might share a story about shopping for apples, and ask, "Now, what does this teach us about our food supply?"

When I think of framing, of careful selection of detail and of mental clarity, I think of Vermeer. His paintings give us a shimmering view of a well-defined world. And yet he lived in a time of wars, pestilence, and chaos. The calmness and order in Vermeer's art did not exist in his country at that time. He created it by his framing.

TONE

Tone is the emotional timbre of speech or writing. It is not everything, but it matters a great deal. As Mark Twain wrote, "Calmness is a language that the blind can read and the deaf can hear." Clients arrive overwrought, overwhelmed, and anxious. Often, the therapist's first step is to settle clients down. Only then can they reflect.

As change agents in our loud, fast, high-intensity culture, we can accomplish much the same thing as Vermeer did by sharing calm, reasoned writing. We can invite readers into a place that feels safe and accepting and offer them the conditions and experiences that they need in order to grow and connect with others.

Thich Nhat Hanh tells a story about the Vietnamese who escaped by boats across the South China Sea. They were often caught in severe weather, and many passengers panicked and made things even more dangerous by running back and forth. In these desperate circumstances, captains discovered that if just one person stayed calm, everyone would calm down, thus making the boat safer. In a sense, all people are riding a rickety boat across dangerous seas. I like to think of writers as the steady ones saying, "Breathe deeply, stay steady, we will make it if we help one another."

While tone is one of the foundations of change writing, many writers focus on content and word choice and almost totally ignore tone. Like voice, tone is individual. I encourage you to practice writing the same set of ideas in different tones. Study your work to develop a sense for the emotions you convey on paper. Notice how you feel as you write. And when you read letters to the editor, op-ed pieces, transformational fiction, or other change writing, study the tone. Once you begin looking for tonal aspects of writing, you will spot them everywhere. The more conscious you are of this aspect of writing, the more effective your writing will be.

TIMING

In therapy and writing, as with jokes and melons, timing is critical. Therapists try to make points at exactly the moment clients are ready to hear them. Too early and it zips over the client's head; too late and the point is irrelevant. This is true of writing as well. Many writers raced ahead of their time and were appreciated only decades later. While a great deal of writing repeats conventional wisdom and does nothing to move the zeitgeist along, effective change-agent writing has an intuitive sense for the profound and momentous in the person or culture. They anticipate when there will be an interesting turning.

We want our ideas to hit the streets when people are receptive to them but before they are too obvious. As with surfers, writers want to be in the exact right place at exactly the right time—on top of the wave, ready to move out just as it crests. Ideally, readers will react to the writing with "I was just ready to think of that myself" or "I didn't know how much I cared about this until I read your work."

Dealing with Darkness

We live lives that are hopelessly broken and we know it.

—PAUL TILLICH

I don't need to read the news, I see it on the faces of everyone I meet.   —GREG BROWN

One time, when I was driving down the street in downtown Boulder, Colorado, a deer careened past my car. He looked to be older, lost and disoriented. His eyes shone with fear, and his tongue lolled out to one side like a thirsty dog's. As he tried to navigate through traffic, he crashed into cars. Many drivers and pedestrians felt sorry for him, but none of us knew how to help. A teenager finally called the police on his cell phone. When the light changed, I gently eased past the deer, feeling his anguish in my own body.

Sometimes, I feel like that deer: lost, confused, frightened, and alone. I am careening through an environment I do not understand but sense is deeply dangerous. I want to find my peaceful green home but don't know how. No one nearby can tell me. I wonder if we all don't feel like that deer at times, all yearning to round up our families, tear up our streets and buildings, and run for our forest homes.

Guilt, fear, envy, anger, and despair—these are the dark emotions. By now, I have worked with sex offenders and murderers, some of whom felt no guilt, and also with clients who felt guilty a dozen times a minute. I have handed Kleenex to women who spoke of rapes and childhood sexual abuse. I have listened as people shouted terrible things at family members. Darkness is part of the great "suchness" of the universe. And I am religious enough to believe that it is here to teach us something.

I am sympathetic to the Buddhist conception that terrible behavior is unskilled behavior that comes from ignorance. As bell hooks wrote, "Everything terrible is really something helpless that needs help from us." Unacknowledged emotions do not disappear; they fester. Ignoring dark emotions leads to addiction and violence. In fact, most of the truly rotten behavior in the world comes from running away from feelings.

For therapists and writers, the first steps in working with darkness involve simply acknowledging it and trying to understand it. Intense dark emotions have inspired some of the best writing. Mark Twain, Charles Dickens, Victor Hugo, and Frederick Douglass, for example, all translated rage into effective writing that eventually led to cultural change. Work is a superb anodyne for despair. As Joe Hill said just before he was executed for his union activities, "Don't mourn, organize."

RESISTANCE

Therapists learn that clients both fear and long to be known. Everyone likes progress but resists change. Even desperate people who pay for advice are not all that willing to take it. Skilled therapists know that it is generally better to deflect arguments than to win them.

Often, in the real world, people who behave badly or disagree with others are shamed or made to feel guilty. However, shame and guilt are poor motivating tools. They sap energy, and lead to rigid thinking. They may work short-term, but long-term they almost never sustain good behavior.

Usually, therapists are most effective when they appeal to their clients' better selves. In Alcoholics Anonymous, for example, people often are transformed by their experiences on the hot seat. Most alcoholics sit rigidly unmoved through the criticism part, but then they melt when pelted with love and approval. Compassion and acceptance, especially self-forgiveness, open up thinking and allow for growth.

Cynicism is a form of resistance, a walling off of the possibilities for transformation. At its core, it is a response to learned helplessness, a defensive strategy. Scratch every cynic and underneath you find a wounded idealist. For therapists and writers alike, the best treatment for cynicism is healing stories.

We therapists sometimes tell stories about ourselves, but only if they will help our clients move forward. Healing stories are not for or about us, and they are not just entertaining. They are fables, cautionary tales, teaching tools. Change writers utilize stories in much the same way, to give people an emotional experience that opens their hearts and points them in new directions.

As persuasive writers, we can overcome readers' resistance by anchoring our issues in the experiences of real people. If we write, in traditional ways, about raising the minimum wage, people will have their usual political, knee-jerk reactions. We can better inspire action by describing the family life of a single mother who subsists on the minimum wage. Readers may be moved by her suffering, and identify her as someone like themselves, and want to do something to help. One of the simplest and most effective ways to move readers to action is to create for them a story about the conditions that moved us to care.

As writers, we want to demystify the change process. Especially when dealing with such monoliths as multinational corporations and government bureaucracy, most Americans are reluctant to act. Yet we can suggest that just as Americans brush their teeth and do their dishes, so they can work a few minutes for their own causes as part of being a citizen.

In both therapy and writing, we want to help people see the connections between their actions and consequences of those actions. For example, in *A Cafecito Story* Julia Alvarez connects coffee production to the lives of peasants in Central America. She and her husband purchased a small plantation in the Dominican Republic, and provided the families who worked there with vegetable gardens, a school, and a medical facility. On the plantation, they did not use pesticides or harsh fertilizers that would leach into the water table. Alvarez then compares their small plantation with others owned by large corporations. Once I understood the connection between my shopping habits and the loss of songbirds, I changed my coffee-buying behavior. I couldn't keep to my old brands. Consciousness raising is irreversible.

Asking people to monitor a specific aspect of their lives or their culture can be an effective form of intervention. Therapists ask clients to count how many times a week they have fun or do a good

deed, or gamble or shout at their kids. Just quantifying events in-
creases awareness and enhances potential for change. Every day,
newspapers, radios, and televisions report news from the business
world, including the Dow Jones and NASDAQ averages. But we do
not have regular reports that give us the statistics for depleted
species, polluted water tables, or deaths from asthma. Or even the
number of people who died alone. If we did, we might pay more attention to these phenomena.

It takes practice to know when to push forward and when to pull
back, and also how to motivate others to take that first step. Once
people do, the work itself becomes reinforcing. Action is the governor of the system. Psychological research demonstrates that people
are more likely to "behave" their way into thinking than to "think"
their way into behaving. We smile and are happier. We whistle in the
dark and feel less afraid. As a therapist, I usually suggest action. Start
studying for the GED. Schedule a physical. Start adoption proceed-
ings. Ask your boss for a raise. Take a five-minute minivacation every
day. Tell your parents you love them. When people do these things,
their attitudes change.

As change writers, we can offer readers ideas for action. If readers take our advice to work in a soup kitchen for the homeless, they
are likely to become more sympathetic toward the poor. We humans
are hardwired to care for what we love, but we also come to love
what we learn to care for.

Remember, readers want these suggestions. A friend told me she
had just read a book on human trafficking. She was heartbroken to
realize how widespread it was, even in the United States. But she was
angry at the book's author. She told me, "I finished that book and I
was ready to move on this issue. The author didn't give one suggestion or idea about what I could do."

Begin the journey with baby steps. Depressed or anxious clients cannot do much at first, but they can do a little. For a woman afraid of men and dating, I might suggest that she watch men at her workplace and take notes on their behavior. Then I would encourage her to actually smile at or greet a man, and later to talk briefly with him. Still later, I might ask her to imagine enjoying a successful date with him. Even tiny steps in the right direction can signal a great turning.

HOPE

With dreams come responsibilities. —LANGSTON HUGHES

Connecters help readers imagine a better future. Think of John Lennon's song "Imagine" and the power it holds for people all over the world. Recall Martin Luther King's "I have a dream" speech. Once imagined, dreams become possibilities.

As a therapist, I try to help clients see that change is possible, that chinks of light are always breaking through the gloom. One of my favorite phrases as a therapist was "Up until now." When a client said "I'm not a hard worker" or "Nobody likes me" or "I have no sense of humor," I would respond, "Up until now."

Progress is almost never linear and easy; rather, it is loopy and arduous. Often, it is hard to know what is good news and what is bad. A man may show up for a root canal and end up marrying the dentist. A woman may be fired from her job and two weeks later land a better one.

Therapists predict these ups and downs. They say, "No doubt you will have moments when you don't think this is helping. That's to be expected." Or, "Setbacks are natural. Ride them out and keep on trucking." Writers can say, "You may grow discouraged as you try to change." Or, "You may not be able to do everything, but you can do something."

I tell my writing students the story of a friend who had given up on his writing. He had received minimal encouragement and been published only in small journals. Eventually, he decided he was deluding himself that he could write. He dropped out of his writing circles, moved, and went to work in public relations. Years later, he was browsing in a used book store in San Francisco and saw that one of his stories had been published in a collection of the best short stories of that year. Immediately, my friend quit public relations and resumed writing. He is now a successful writer, with works published in translation all over the world.

ORCHESTRATING MOMENTS

As a therapist, I approached sessions with a sense of direction, a set of skills, and an eagerness to understand. My standard techniques assisted many clients through rough patches, yet magic, by definition something intangible, ineffable, and hard to pin down, is what causes transformation. People do not change unless they have a powerful emotional turning. This may be through epiphanies, insights, or deep connecting moments between the people in the room. Over time, I have grown more inclined to set aside my plans and embrace whatever is happening at the moment. Working with the here and now often produces the freshest lessons.

As writers, we know that epiphanies and surprise visits by the muse give our writing energy and beauty. Even a rather prosaic piece, once touched by magic, glows with a whole new light. We are transformed by these moments of grace, and, when we share them with readers, they often are transformed as well.

As change agents, both writers and therapists want to engineer situations that allow this type of moment to occur. Epiphanies cannot be scheduled, but they can be invited. Think of Buddha under the bodhi tree, Jesus in the garden of Gethsemane, or Allah on the road to Mecca. Different religions employ different language to describe these moments. To the Buddhist, it is enlightenment. To Christians, a state of grace. And to Muslims, rahman. Yet all religions seek to evoke times when true believers are fully present, open to the universe, and filled with awe.

Facilitating a change process in clients or readers often involves orchestrating situations that allow for aha experiences. Therapists cannot force the experience, but they can arrange for silence, beauty, and heart-softening moments—all of which foster epiphanies. And while writers can tell stories that change the lives of readers, they also can recommend experiences that allow epiphanies to occur, such as lying on a beach, listening to the waves and seabirds, and watching the clouds waft across the sky.

Writing and therapy are both about creating the conditions that allow us to take people to the mountain. When people's breathing changes and their eyes fill with wonder, they will walk down that mountain ready to perform miracles.

EIGHT

SWIMMING ALONG—THE WRITING PROCESS

> We live in an occupied country, misunderstood. Justice will take us millions of intricate moves.   —WILLIAM STAFFORD
>
> Why not just tell the truth?   —RAYMOND CARVER

Writing from the Heart

I wrote *Another Country* after my mother's death. My mother had not had an easy time of dying. She spent her last eleven months in a hospital, hooked up to machines, pumped full of drugs, and, finally, unable to move, eat, or speak. I lived in another state, and was torn between caring for my own family and being with my mother. For a year, no matter where I was, I felt guilty, and, no matter how hard I worked, I was never doing enough. I discovered that nothing in our culture was organized to make my mother's death or my taking care of her easy. I felt strongly that our country could do a better job helping adult children and their dying parents. While I had learned lessons too late for my mother and me, I hoped my writing about this time in my life would help others.

Writing requires so much energy and focus that I can't imagine writing about subjects that have no personal importance for me. Without emotions fueling the process, where does the energy come from? Awe prompts writing, as does great joy or even rage. People who have experienced terrible events or suffered greatly often burn with a desire to record them; many of their books are what the French call a *cri de coeur,* a cry from the heart. They remind me of Willa Cather's famous quote, "It's easy to be a writer. You just open a vein and bleed over every page."

Anna Akhmatova, a Russian poet from the Stalinist era, would stand in a line of women at a prison in Moscow, day after cold, snowy day. They were waiting to see family members who had been incarcerated by Stalin for the most imaginary of crimes. Hungry, freezing, and exhausted, the women were humiliated by the guards, forced to pay bribes, and often turned away. On one particularly dreadful morning, a woman admonished Akhmatova: "You must tell others what is happening here. The world must know this." That admonition became Akhmatova's moral assignment, and she incorporated the incident into one of her most famous poems.

Many people have powerful stories but lack the skills to be powerful writers. Writers need to be skilled or, when the heart speaks, it is the language of sentimental schmaltz. Yet skill alone is not sufficient. We need authentic emotion to go with it. Powerful writing includes sparkling details, apt metaphors, surprises, and restraint. It has tones and rhythms that change like those of a symphony. The best writing causes readers' breathing to change.

Writing from the heart does not always come from loving feelings. When we see something we love being badly treated, we are motivated to write because of rage. Occasionally, we can use such anger to persuade, but that requires self-control. While rage that is contained creatively can be useful, cathartic writing generally bombs. Theologian Reinhold Niebuhr wrote that to effect change, we need to practice "spiritual discipline against resentment."

Writers are sometimes cursed with too much certitude. Especially as activists, many of us are prone to jump on one white horse after another to lead the charge. We may indeed be right; however, we are also likely to be shot. Furthermore, absolute certainty can morph all too easily into rigidity. As Thich Nhat Hanh wrote, "If you have a gun, you can shoot one, two, three, five people; but if you have an ideology and stick to it, thinking it is the absolute truth, you can kill millions."

Absolute certainty can make us unlikable narrators. Preachiness is off-putting, as is too much confidence in our own purity. We want to temper our moral fervor by remembering that our readers may not think like we do, and, hence, will not find our certainty all that appealing. We are more likable narrators if we present ourselves as curious students rather than as smug experts. Humility is appealing.

With the best writing, readers discover something new about themselves. Bob Dylan said it well: "Protest songs are difficult to write without making them come off as preachy and one-dimensional. You have to show people a side of themselves they didn't know is there."

To write honestly and well about emotions, we must push language to its limits. English does not include many words to describe mixed emotions—"poignant" and "bittersweet" are the only two that come to mind. German strings together adjectives to label complicated emotions; Japanese has many words to unsnarl such feelings. Feelings come and go at lightning speed, and we need not resolve them. One of the best things we can do with our mixed emotions is simply describe them. We can express both confusion and sorrow. We can evoke what Wallace Stegner called "the unbroken doublesong of love and lamentation." Our readers understand mixed emotions. They experience them too.

Voyage of Discovery

We write to discover what we think.   —JOAN DIDION

If we are not discovering new territory as we write, we will not be able to offer our readers fresh vistas. The two oldest stories in the world may well be someone leaves town to go on a journey, and a stranger comes to town. In a sense, all writing is travel writing. We are saying to our readers, Come with me to a place I have seen, or, Discover new territory with me, or, I am new in town, and, wow, this is quite a place.

My aunt Margaret drew a good distinction once when she described someone as having led an interesting life but not having been an interesting person. The difference is story. My father could turn a trip to the city dump into an epic tale. On the other hand, I have fought back yawns while listening to people tell of their visit to China, or even their escape from a mountain lion. They just didn't have the knack for making their material intriguing and memorable, what musicians might call "hummable."

Use Everything

Catch an eyeful, catch an earful, then don't drop what you've caught.   —WILLIAM CARLOS WILLIAMS

Use the conversation this morning with your sister, the article on page three of the local newspaper, or the way a mother at the playground disciplines her toddler. Use the way a brother's arm curls around his sister's shoulder as he walks her across a street. Use the high school boy with blue hair holding open a door for the lady in a sweat suit. Use your own feelings of sorrow and guilt as you walk past a homeless schizophrenic man. Use your joy when taking your children fishing. Make use of your daily routine, overheard conservations, your quirkiest thoughts, your dreams, and your most profound revelations.

As a novice, I sometimes thought, This is so good I should save it for later. I never do that now. I have learned to be a spendthrift. I know that good ideas beget good ideas, just as energy begets energy and love begets love. If the process is right, and the neurons are snapping, ideas will burst forth. More gold will come my way.

Advancing an Argument

An argument is the logical progression of valid and clear points that advances a particular point of view. The logic of the argument must command respect. The central point of the argument must march across each page, with each sentence and each paragraph moving it forward. When we build such arguments, we present our readers with important and intellectually exciting writing. And later, if we speak publicly about our ideas, we find them relatively easy to defend.

A good way to approach an argument is to share the circumstances that led us to explore an area in the first place and how we came to the conclusions we did. We can include our own puzzlement, questions, and evidence to the contrary. Readers will start to feel curious along with us. Sometimes, writers confuse repetition with argument. Saying the same thing ten different ways is not advancing an argument. Neither is emphatic speech.

Sometimes we can buttress our arguments by invoking common sense or the highly respected arguments of others. For example, if we are writing as a pacifist, we might say, "Common sense tells us that if we didn't spend money on war, we would have more for food, shelter, medicine, and education." Or if we are advocating Turn Off Your TV week, we might appeal to widely held beliefs: "All good parents want their children to have a childhood, a protected emotional space in which to love, learn, and play." Then we could argue that television violates that protected space. Or if we are arguing for more funding for evacuees of Hurricane Katrina, we could cite Franklin Roosevelt and the establishment of Social Security benefits and New Deal projects as evidence that Americans take care of one another.

Perhaps the easiest way to persuade is to share our own reversals in thinking. Writing "I once thought X, but now, because of Y, I think the opposite" will capture any reader's attention. We can question and refute our own points. We can write, "Cynics might say that . . ." Or "Reasonable people might disagree but . . ." If we can't answer our own questions and back up our own refutations, then we haven't yet constructed a solid argument.

Writing is like building a house. The most critical part is constructing the foundation. Building a solid foundation takes the most time, but, if done properly, finishing the house is simple. Paint the walls, hang the window treatments. By the end, small efforts at prettifying go a long way toward making the house beautiful; with a strong foundation, it may well stand for a hundred years.

Original Thought

The secret of having good ideas is to have a lot of ideas, then throw away the bad ones.   —LINUS PAULING

The race in writing is not to the swift but to the original.
—WILLIAM ZINSSER

The fastest way to write is to pretend you have all the time in the world.   —PHILIP GERARD

Writing is not for the faint of heart. To be successful, writers must say something better, different, or first. We want our writing to unfurl in an organic way. Ideally, we come to trust the present moment as our teacher.

When we are lucky, we enter what the poet Marjorie Saiser calls "cruise control." It is a state of grace, in which our egos have disappeared, the juices are flowing, and we are one with the writing. Musicians and athletes call it "going into the zone." Often, this most effortless of writing ends up being our best work.

While plodding through an argument, we may find ourselves

abruptly taking flight and soaring into a stream of poetry or personal reverie. We should follow this impulse to soar. If we are too task oriented, we can be tempted to ignore these "diversions," yet they are often where the riches lie. Later, we can sort it all out.

We want to train ourselves to follow weird ideas or tangents and see what happens. Often the nagging doubts, the "yes buts," are important clues that something is off. Small inconsistencies, when explored, often reveal big gaps in logic. What seems like a peripheral thought, if pursued, unravels a poorly constructed argument. It prompts us to build a much stronger argument.

Dissenting voices inside our heads often have profound points to make. For example, when I was writing *Reviving Ophelia,* I harbored a set of notions about how the world worked. I soon realized that these notions did not fit with my own observations. In the field of psychology at that time, the main theory about troubled girls was that they came from dysfunctional families. Yet the girls I was seeing were often the brightest and the best. Their parents were willing to devote time and money for therapy to help them. I began looking elsewhere for dysfunction—at school, among peers, and in the popular culture.

Another puzzler was the discrepancy between the gains of the women's movement and the growing unhappiness of young girls. I would have predicted that girls in the 1980s and '90s would be better adjusted than girls from my mother's generation, or even my own 1960s generation, a time when women were shut out of many schools and jobs. But it wasn't so. To unravel this disquieting contradiction, I had to turn to the broader culture of advertising, television, movies, music, and MTV.

Finally, I had expected that girls from tolerant, progressive families would be the best adjusted; instead, girls from conservative, religious families seemed to be more emotionally sturdy. Gradually, I realized that this phenomenon also was related to pop culture. Strict families with strong values protected their daughters from the worst of the environment, giving them real childhoods. The factors that did not fit my preconceived notions ended up as the central arguments of my book. When we writers rethink conventional wisdom, we are helping our readers rethink it as well.

Borders

Everything really interesting and powerful happens at borders. Borders teem with life, color, and complexity. In nature, we find the most diversity where different ecosystems merge. We call these places "edge habitats." Think about the borders between things—between the U.S. and Mexico, between history and geography, between science and art, between childhood and adulthood, between men and women. Edge habitats are a good place to look for material.

Combining different sources can be catalytic. Energy is released. Many of the memorable books of the last century were the result of new combinations: breast cancer and the Great Salt Lake (*Refuge* by Terry Tempest Williams), corporate culture and tribalism (*The Lexus and the Olive Tree* by Thomas Friedman), or biology and philosophy (*The Immense Journey* by Loren Eiseley).

Lively writing often integrates information from many different sources. Even a short piece can combine literary references, quotes, homey stories, science, and theology. We can combine personal and professional experiences, or we can compare people across time. One of my favorite strategies is showing that people from hundreds or even thousands of years ago experienced many of the same problems as people today. That kind of time travel helps me and my readers keep things in perspective.

Precision

> If a writer could truly capture the life of any person for just one day, that writer would be the best writer who ever lived.
>
> —TOLSTOY
>
> Daily life is always extraordinary when rendered precisely.
>
> —BONNIE FRIEDMAN

Precision with details involves the selection and leveraging of images to create intensity and meaning. Any scene we describe offers a multiplicity of choices in terms of details. We are precise when we choose the best details for our pieces.

We all process the world through our bodies. In a profound sense, our bodies are what we have in common. Readers know what dirt smells like after a rain. They know the taste of coffee or summer tomatoes. They know the sound of a baby laughing and a train whistle. They know about the color and dance of burning candles. And they know how it feels to be kissed. When we write about our human experiences, we connect with our readers.

Precision often calls for the replacement of generic terms with chunkier ones. "VW bus" elicits a clearer image than "vehicle," and it may reveal something about our story's character. Remember, it's not the detail itself but the meaning of the detail that is important. There is no reason to describe the elegant furniture in a general's office unless you are commenting on the general's sensibilities or personal wealth.

The way a teenager skulks into a room, the taste of hummus, the texture of corn silk, the smell of gardenias, or the call of geese—we writers can direct readers to experience all of these details in a certain way by our emphasis, tone, and context. A stuffed frog in a child's room can mean quite different things depending on whether the child is healthy or not. The tone with which one discusses a marching band, or even the scent of grape gum, certainly can shape readers' perceptions and reactions.

Description should be in the service of the emotional tone of a piece. Weather, for example, is often about tone. A sunny spring day with cardinals singing evokes a hope-filled or happy tone. We might choose to describe that kind of weather when writing about a girl winning a scholarship to art camp. Or weather can be used for contrast, or to heighten irony or pathos. For example, a woman driving home from the hospital after her husband's death might note the gorgeous April weather in a way that only deepens her sorrow.

As change writers, we want to select details that engage readers with new ideas or groups, or that helps them care about what we care about. We can employ details to tell the reader, I am like you. The editor who bought my proposal for *Reviving Ophelia* later told me that she was moved by a single detail: a girl in therapy crying about a rape as she hugged her teddy bear. Often a precise observation—a glass of red wine spilled on a bedside table, or an old couple hobbling along a hiking trail—is what nails the point.

Odd juxtapositions make for compelling writing. Once I visited a slum where the dismal shacks were plastered with newsprint photographs of expensive appliances, BMWs, and luxury vacation resorts, which seemed to mock the inhabitants. Another time, standing in an ICU beside a friend who lay dying of emphysema, I heard the nurses discussing the best pizza joints in town. Notice such juxtapositions in your life and write them down. They are often powerful and poignant, and they add depth to your writing.

Bertrand Russell once wrote, "The mark of a civilized human being is the capacity to read a column of numbers and weep." Some people can respond to numbers. The six million killed in the Holocaust has deep meaning for many of us. Certainly, most Americans are saddened by the number of dead from the war in Iraq or the earthquake in Kashmir. And, of course, many change writers need facts and accurate statistics in their work. Without the proper documentation, our arguments and stories lack context, perspective, or credibility.

Yet humans are not adding machines. We are experience-seeking, story-seeking organisms. Stories make people laugh or weep because they engage the sensory and emotional systems of our bodies. I urge you to be selective and parsimonious in your use of numbers or statistics. Most readers quickly grow bored with them. As Stalin put it, "If you kill one man it's murder, if you kill a million it is a statistic."

Subtlety

In art, economy is always beauty.   —HENRY JAMES

Truth is best achieved by suggestion.   —WILLA CATHER

Really big ideas—such as God, death, love, and honor—often can be best tackled indirectly. Once, on an airplane, I watched an older woman carry on a homemade angel food cake. She held it on her lap for the whole three-hour flight, and I could tell that whoever was receiving that cake was loved. Death can be effectively discussed by describing a child sitting beside an empty chair, a Thanksgiving without grandmother's noodles, or a black suit taken from the hall closet.

We need not beat people over the head with our ideas. Readers are quick learners. Subtlety allows them to imagine, to fill in the blanks, and thus to be involved in the creative work in progress. Especially when we are dealing with emotional material, less can be more. Chekhov wrote, "When you wish to move your reader to pity, be colder."

Often we writers are taking our readers to a place no one really wants to go—into a discussion of autistic children, the worldwide AIDS crisis, Darfur, or sex slaves. We are asking them to be upset and sad. They will only follow us if they trust us. If our readers shut down in horror, they will stop reading. We need to leverage our relationship with readers so that we can tell them things that are hard to hear.

Metaphors

Metaphors are paths into something much deeper and older than we are. They are one of the most powerful ways to express the wholeness of our ideas. We want our metaphors sparkling, apt, and rich enough that they can be extended throughout our pieces.

Clumsy metaphors lead readers astray. And we can be trapped by our own metaphors. We need to watch out for ones that come too easily, or that frame the world in ways we do not want it framed. War metaphors tend to be overused. I avoid them because I generally do not want to frame life as a battle. To explore the implications of metaphors, think of all the possible ways you could frame life—as a train ride, a shopping trip, a movie, a quest, or maybe a quilt or a hayrack ride in October. Then note how those frames can lead to different philosophical positions.

Be aware that age, gender, and class biases may be embedded in your metaphors. Sports metaphors are an example of this type of bias. A metaphor that depends on readers' knowledge of cricket is likely to elude most people. While metaphors related to birds and flowers are apt for me, they are likely to lose most urban eighteen-year-olds. Likewise, a metaphor that compares life to a Club Med resort could irritate people who barely can afford a vacation to a nearby state park.

Originally, I called this chapter "A Tool Kit for Writers." Now, that's probably a decent metaphor for someone who actually works with tools. In fact, Ted Kooser used this metaphor to marvelous effect in his book *The Poetry Home Repair Manual.* But I couldn't riff on it at all; when I tried, I sounded hackneyed and fake. But swimming—now, that is the metaphor for me. I can easily combine my experiences of swimming and writing.

Organizing Paper

More often than we like to admit, writing is organizing paper. Computer files, book recommendations, academic articles, names of people to contact for information, old writing, and dream fragments—all these things must be organized and properly stored. In a library, a book misfiled is a book lost. With writers, an idea misfiled is an idea lost.

We want to take the time to carefully plan and implement a storage and retrieval system. Ideally, we build a system that allows us easy access to our snips of writing, beloved quotations, and saved information from decades earlier. Most of us don't quite succeed, but our best efforts mean less material lost and less time searching for papers.

Sometimes, something we wrote years ago is just what your friends want you to read at their wedding. Or perhaps a cut we made in a speech or sermon is just what we require for an upcoming speech. Who among us hasn't spent a whole day trying to find something we wrote long ago? Often, thoughts from yesteryear are surprisingly apt. After all, we each have a limited number of interests, struggles, and life themes. Seasoned writers learn to not throw much away. We are good recyclers.

We all develop our own ways of organizing our scraps of thought. I carry a little notebook at all times, and anytime I see, hear, or think something interesting I write it down. I write down new or odd words, conversations, engaging details, book ideas, stories that move me, unusual juxtapositions, and phone numbers of people I might want to ask questions of later.

When I arrive home, I file these notes. I know that many people organize information on their computers, and, at a certain point, so do I. However, I developed my organizing skills before I owned a computer, and I haven't felt a need to fix what isn't broken. I continue to use notebooks, file cards, manila folders, desk drawers, and file cabinets—all very low-tech. If I dropped dead tomorrow, no one else could figure out my system. However, I know how it works, right down to the labeled boxes of mail and old papers stored in banana boxes in my closet.

I keep a notebook of books to be read, with gold stars next to the ones relevant to my current work. I also have a bookcase filled with books on writing, with relevant points underlined. I have old journals dating back to 1977. Yet I managed to lose one of the most important pieces of my writing: my white leather diary from junior high. I would pay a lot of money today for that little book. I would love to have a trail to follow into my life and thoughts as a young girl. If you are young enough to heed this advice for yourself or your children, save every journal and poem from schooldays on. It's amazing how useful childhood writing can be, not only for writing but also for self-understanding.

I have an entire drawer in an old file cabinet filled with what I consider fresh thoughts. Now and then, one is useful in a surprising way. And, like many writers, I have a file of book and project ideas. I also have a special notebook for metaphors I like, and another for quotes. This level of organization has been no small feat. If you have been writing for decades or are working out of a studio apartment with a mate, two kids, and a cat, I feel your pain. Yet there really is no choice. You can lose years of work and some of your best ideas because you failed to spend fifty bucks on supplies and a week of your time getting organized.

Perhaps now is the time to mention backup. We all know stories of writing lost when computers died, houses burned, or the postman didn't make a delivery. The way to prevent this is backup. When I write on the computer, I always print out a hard copy of what I wrote at the end of my day. I also have backup discs that I store in our shed, far from the house. That way, if a tornado blows our house away, there is at least a chance that the shed will remain standing and my work spared. If you don't have a shed, send copies to a friend or family member. Trust me on this one.

Research

Rumor can run all the way around the world while Truth is still putting on his pants.   —MARK TWAIN

Always make sure you get the moon in the right part of sky.
                                —EUDORA WELTY

Everyone is entitled to his own opinion, but not his own facts.   —DANIEL PATRICK MOYNIHAN

I will not discuss traditional ways to do research—on a home computer, at the library, by interviewing experts or attending lectures—except to underscore the importance of accuracy. We have a moral responsibility to be honest and exact. Furthermore, small mistakes cause readers to mistrust us. They think, If the author doesn't know this, why should I assume she knows that? Particularly if what we are writing about is controversial, people who disagree with us will first challenge our facts. We want to document and be able to defend the statistics we use.

But knowing the facts is easier said than done. True, the moon rises in the east. But what vitamins should we take? Are yearly mammograms necessary? Are there really more autistic kids in the United States now than in the past? How many civilian casualties have there been in Afghanistan?

Facts can turn out to be slippery little critters. Unless put into proper perspective, they can easily mislead us. My Republican daughter-in-law and I agreed that if we traded books, news channels, and magazine subscriptions for a year, we would both most likely re-configure our positions. There is enough information out there to justify almost any argument.

Once, I made a speech at a university in a state where beef was the main industry. I spoke about abuses of refugees in some meatpacking and processing plants. A donor to the school who owned a major beef-packing corporation was upset by my remarks. She wrote me a letter questioning the statistics I had quoted from Eric Schlosser's *Fast Food Nation* and my local newspaper. We both had our "facts" and our "science." They just weren't the same facts and science.

My favorite kind of research comes from what I call the satura-tion/immersion method. When I write a book, I move into the ter-ritory of my subject and park myself there until I'm finished. I read literature and academic work relevant to my work. With *The Middle of Everywhere,* I read the stories of immigrants and refugees, as well as local newspaper articles about newcomers. And I listened to music from refugee countries, and saw movies about refugees, and at-tended ethnic festivals and religious celebrations.

I join the community I am studying as a connected critic. With *The Middle of Everywhere,* I became a culture broker for three families, teaching them how to drive, shop, enroll in school, access health care, find jobs, and deal with the Immigration and Naturalization Service. I attended meetings and workshops, parties, healing rituals, even a birth. For two years, I lived in the world of newcomers. I tried to keep up on immigration laws, politics, geography, and history from the countries of our refugees. I read about cross-cultural men-tal health and trauma treatment. I interviewed judges, police, public health nurses, and teachers who worked with refugees.

Interviews

Interviews and observations are powerful forms of research. I have learned a great deal sitting in on classes at schools, or with elders in nursing home dining rooms. Some of my best ideas have cropped up when I was watching kids and their parents at a church fun night, or picnicking with Kurdish refugees.

While statistical research and control-group studies are published in journals more frequently, the most groundbreaking work often has come from the careful observation of small samples. Freud, Jung, Piaget, and Alice Miller carefully observed individual patients, and these relatively few observations led them to theories about humans in general. Science moves forward because of statistically significant research. But it also moves forward because of observation and eureka moments.

For me, interviewing is not a linear process. I do not gather information and then write a book. I interact with people all the way through the writing process. I advance hypotheses, then conduct interviews to verify them, then develop more sophisticated hypotheses. Starting out, I often conduct some interviews to determine the lay of the land, then, later, other interviews to understand nuances or fill in gaps. Toward the end of a project, I often have more sophisticated and focused questions to explore, so I will schedule a few last-minute interviews to get answers.

Writers can locate interviewees informally, even randomly. We can ask friends for referrals and introductions, be they business-people, police officers, or workers in rehab units. Often, we can find people to interview by contacting institutions, taking an ad out in the newspaper, or making a speech about our subject of interest and asking the audience to sign up for interviews. Most people are eager to offer their opinions. We all want to be heard.

While we want to interview a variety of people, soliciting too many stories that make similar points can overwhelm us later with overlapping material. While we want to go into interviews well prepared, we also want to be poised for the spontaneous. We want to know what is unique about our interviewees and yet we want them to answer the same questions we are asking everyone else.

With my books about demographic groups, such as teenagers or the elderly, I ask interviewees if they want me to use their real names, and I honor their preferences. In certain situations, such as when I write about therapy clients, I use composites. It is critical that we report honestly to our readers how we have handled names.

Before we begin our interviews, we need to explain who we are, why we are doing what we are doing, and how our information will be used. We need to discuss confidentiality and release forms. I ask interviewees to look at these forms before the interview but not to decide whether to sign them until after. Sometimes, publishers supply release forms, but I draw up my own, very simple ones.

I never try to coax anyone into participating in an interview. If people have doubts about being interviewed, I withdraw quickly and gracefully. Partly, it's a matter of respect. But it's also a highly adaptive defense for me. Ambivalent subjects are more likely to make trouble later. Of course, in some cases you may have no choice. If you are writing about a toxic waste dump, you need to interview the CEO of the company doing the dumping.

Before commencing the interview, we want to invite questions and concerns. Once we are under way, we want to be quiet and let our subjects talk. If we are control freaks, we will miss the gold. We want to attend the emotions, watch our subjects' faces, and note the sighs and the silences. We shouldn't leap to fill in the pauses, but rather should stay still and see what unfurls. As a character in Joan Silber's book *Ideas of Heaven* put it, "Shutting up is a good research tool."

We want to tune into energy, passion, and powerful and unique ideas. We want to attend to repeating themes, metaphors, and unusual language. We want to fathom the meaning behind the words. As we listen, we ask ourselves, How has this person been changed by his experiences? How has he grown? Slow is actually fast with interviewing. A calm, all-the-time-in-the-world demeanor elicits the most interesting, usable information. The most personal information is likely to be shared just as we say good-bye, when we think the interview is over.

Most writers love research, but we can overdo it. Notebooks full of information, dozens of interviews, files of contacts, and shelves of books can be overwhelming when it comes time to write the book. A rich experience base makes our manuscript denser, more vivid, and more reflective of diverse and complex reality. But there comes a day when it's time to stop researching and start selecting and integrating. We will always find room for critical new information, but we reach a point where more is not better. Enough already.

The Accordion Method

When I wrote my first book, I invented a way to make my work denser and tighter. The accordion method alternates cycles of expanding and contracting manuscripts. In the expansion phase, I toss in every idea, quotation, story, and tangent that comes to me and build up to a huge, ungainly behemoth that is rich in hypotheses and lively details. I even let it overwhelm me with its sheer size. Then I start to contract it. First, I make some judgments about what is core to my project. I cut by half, removing ideas not relevant to the central theme. I delete the dull, reorganize, then delete some more. When I have a lean, spare draft, I begin a new expansion phase, and add new ideas, quotations, stories, and tangents.

The accordion method is time-consuming, and requires self-discipline bordering on masochism. However, it works for me. Repeating this process, squeezing my work tightly, then expanding it widely, intensifies the work's power and richness. You might want to give it a try.

In this chapter on process, I have assumed that you have dived into your project and are warmed up, and that your breathing has become slow and regular. You are deeply immersed in a world of currents and wavering light. You have forgotten entirely the solid world. Time has vanished.

Then the doorbell rings. Your neighbor comes by for your weekly coffee together, or your family walks through the front door. Or your boss calls, and asks you to come into the office. You emerge from your writing somewhat dazed. The writing environment feels more real than the one you return to. Most likely, you want to stay in the water. But as you reengage with the world, you are likely to feel refreshed and invigorated. Tomorrow, you will return to your desk and examine your work. You will begin to revise.

NINE

POINT OF VIEW

Infinite nuances are needed if justice is to be done to individual human beings.   —CARL JUNG

The rocks in the water don't know how the rocks in the sun feel.   —HAITIAN PROVERB

In the Lotus Sutra, a sacred text of Mahayana Buddhism, a holy person named "Wondrous Sound" is able to speak to each person in his or her own language. To someone who can hear music, he sings. To someone who speaks the language of the street, he speaks the language of the street. Every word is uttered in a way that opens the listener to transformation.

All therapists are in training to be Wondrous Sound bodhisattvas. Therapy can be defined as the art of understanding another person's point of view and then utilizing that knowledge to be helpful to that person. Change writing almost always involves trying to understand the points of view of others and communicating those points of view to readers. For me, this attempt at understanding is the most profound connection between therapy and writing.

Point of view involves a time, a place, and an observer. It concerns how we direct our attention, where we stand, and what we bring to our observations. It exposes our character structure, motives, personal style, and knowledge of the world. It reveals to readers our intellectual clarity and capacity for empathy.

In a sense, our description of who we observe is always a double portrait. It's about our subject and about our own ways of perceiving and understanding other humans.

Morality is deeply connected to point of view. Moral action depends on understanding the perspective (thoughts, feelings, and experiences) of others. Expanding the number of reference points by which we or our readers view the universe allows for the development of moral imagination. Without this, we humans are incapable of accurate empathy.

Thinking about point of view is an early step in the writing process. Point of view is involved in the decision to walk into the study, pick up a pen, and tackle a particular set of issues. It is the vantage point from which we tell our stories. Choices about it require us to ask who speaks to whom, from what distance, with what limits, and with what goals.

Point of view is not just an issue of craft such as spelling or grammar. It reflects our understanding of the world. Beneath whatever story we write, point of view somehow encompasses our deepest motives and our moral integrity. It does this by revealing in subtle ways why we write what we do, and how we hope to have an impact on the world.

Point of view has at least two different aspects: one involves our relationship to our subject, the other our relationship with readers. For example, when I wrote *The Middle of Everywhere*, about refugees in Nebraska, I had a deeply sympathetic view of my subjects. I also had a point of view about my audience. I assumed they were good-hearted but limited in their knowledge about refugees. I wanted to tell them stories of newcomers, and expand their frames of reference. I hoped that as they read my book, they would be more able to think of refugees as people rather than stereotypes.

Insiders, Outsiders, Connected Critics

Writers can work from three basic positions: intimate insiders, outsiders, or what anthropologist Renato Rosaldo calls "connected critics." This last position is where writers are intimately involved in the lives of their subjects, but also are able to observe them from a somewhat detached vantage point. All three positions have built-in advantages and disadvantages. Insiders sometimes suffer from habituation, and write with blunted perspective. As insiders, we can know too much, and lose ourselves in arcane detail. Or we can be blinded by groupthink, and be inclined to spout the official story.

On the plus side, writing as insiders gives us authority, and allows us to use our knowledge and experience. We have good contacts and easy access to research. Often, we can bring years of reflection and institutional wisdom to our readers. Dr. Ira Byock wrote *Dying Well* as an insider. He had spent seventeen years caring for the dying, serving as hospice director in his hometown and national director of a program to improve end-of-life care. By the time he wrote his book, he had plenty to say.

Our America, by LeAlan Jones and Lloyd Newman, is an insider's story. Jones and Newman, adolescents who lived on the South Side of Chicago in Cabrini Green, carried around tape recorders and interviewed their neighbors about life in the tenements. Because the boys were trusted by area residents, they were able to record intimate, unguarded conversations. Radio producer David Isay gave them the recorders in the first place, and helped them edit and publish their interviews.

When we write as outsiders, we may not know what we are talking about. We may be too unfamiliar with our subject to grasp critical aspects of the situation. I am thinking of the folly of writing about a group one hasn't taken the trouble to get to really know. As an uneducated outsider, we could miss both nuances and the underlying issues.

Yet the great benefit of outsider writing is that it allows us to look at a world with fresh eyes. For example, in *Postville: A Clash of Cultures in Heartland America,* Stephen Bloom visits a small Iowa town to learn how rural midwesterners deal with a large group of Lubavitchers, one of the most orthodox and zealous of Jewish sects. Bloom arrives with certain perceptions and leaves with very different ones. With outsider's eyes, we learn as we go, and readers learn along with us.

My favorite writing often comes from the connected critic point of view. This is a complex perspective to manage technically since we are always struggling with issues of distance and objectivity. We never can stop asking, At this moment, in this scene, where am I standing? The answer, of course, is we are simultaneously standing on the balcony and dancing in the courtyard.

Connected critics seek both the objectivity and connection of good fieldworkers in anthropology. Anthropologists study the community that they have joined, and they become a significant part of a story. Margaret Mead's *Coming of Age in Samoa* is an early example of this perspective. Pictures in the book show Mead in native clothes working alongside village women. She wrote a book that is important enough to still be discussed almost a century later.

Melissa Fay Greene's *Praying for Sheetrock* was written from this point of view. Greene traveled to McIntosh County, Georgia, to interview citizens about racial integration in their town. Her story is of the political awakening of the black community and the downfall of the power elite, a gang of racist thugs. For a time, Greene lived both as an outsider trying to understand the life of the county and an insider as part of the black community. Much as any reporter would, she interviewed everyone she could and reported on their positions. Yet she was not an "objective" journalist because she clearly sided with the black sharecroppers.

Once we have settled into a general point of view, we still will struggle with specifics. What is the right mix of detachment and connection? Will our descriptions of our reactions heighten our readers' involvement or make them doubt our objectivity? Or are we so detached that the writing feels bloodless and clinical?

Another important question to ponder is how much we want the reader to learn about us. Are we important to the story? How much do we tell readers about our relationships with our subjects? If we are health workers writing about the inner city, do we write just what we observe, or do we put ourselves into the scene grieving or raging? Do we say that the boiled yak meat we ate on our trek across Nepal made us ill? Do we confess that we have nothing but scorn for certain government policies? Do we explain that we care about infant mortality because we lost a baby ourselves? The answer to all these questions is: It depends. It depends on what we are trying to achieve, and our own judgments about the best strategies to achieve it.

Using her own reactions to tell a story worked well for Barbara Ehrenreich in her book *Nickle and Dimed.* She writes about what it was like to struggle to live on minimum-wage paychecks and to work in menial jobs. But sometimes, talking about oneself can be a mistake. Some books tell readers more about their authors than readers care to know. Readers can easily judge such authors as self-involved and boring.

When and how much to insert oneself in one's writing is a tricky question that I have struggled with in this book. I've asked, When do I share my own story as a writer? Sometimes my experiences may be helpful to readers, yet too much self-insertion is, well, too much.

How we feel about our subjects—an aspect of point of view—affects the tone we use when we write about them. This is not the same thing as the tone of the piece. For example, I could write an angry piece about injustice about someone I deeply love. When we feel stuck in our writing, this tonal quality toward our subjects can offer us clues about our difficulties. For example, when I was working on *Reviving Ophelia*, I realized that my tone toward my teenage subjects was often harsh, and filled with frustration. I was judging girls for being selfish, shallow, and irresponsible. Then an alarm bell clanged. After all, these were children whose families were seeking my help. What was I missing that I needed to see in order to be more respectful toward them? As I figured that out, I discovered the meaning of my book.

Point of view is not about "should"s. As long as we are conscious of the effects of our decisions on our writing, almost any point of view can work. The more mindful we are of point of view, the more skillful and artful we can be. No one is truly objective. As Ted Kooser wrote, "Your feelings will surface no matter what you are writing." Hear! Hear! We may be logical and rational but all of us have highly personal points of view on the universe. In fact, that is why we have something to say.

Pronouns

Some of our trickiest point-of-view work is deciding whether to use "I," "we," "they," or "you." I had more trouble with pronouns in this book than in any other, perhaps because I wrote it from many vantage points—as a therapist, as a person wanting to be useful to our troubled planet, as a fellow writer, and as a teacher of writing.

When we are in trouble with our pronouns, most likely we haven't sorted out our relationship to readers and/or to our material. We are probably struggling with us/them issues, and questions about the applicability of our remarks to ourselves. For example, I could write a book on skydiving, but it wouldn't apply to me. I have never skydived, nor do I plan to do so. This topic was a different matter. Almost everything I write here applies to my own work.

When we sense pronoun trouble, it's time to slow down and carefully untangle our work. We can address readers as "you," but often imbedded in the you readers is "we," since writers often include themselves in whatever thoughts they are sharing with readers. For example, I could write the following perfectly decent sentence: "You need to act now to stop ad campaigns that encourage children to eat unhealthy foods." A better sentence might begin with "We," to signal that we are all responsible for taking action, myself included.

On the other hand, in this book I can't write, "We who are seeking to be published for the first time . . ." since I have been published. And yet I sound show-offy if I write, "We experienced writers . . ." Or falsely modest if I say, "We novices . . ." In short, "we" can be a challenging pronoun to use gracefully.

It is easy to make assumptions about our readers, but the overuse of "we" can cause readers to resist us. For example, if I begin a sentence with "We women," or "We who are college educated . . . ," I am leaving people out, and I am making assumptions about my readers that may not be justified. Readers may argue with me and even put aside my writing if they sense that I am denying legitimate differences.

Because I value connection, I employ "we" when I can; however, sometimes "you" or "they" are the best choices. In addition, there may be times we do not want to be part of the group we are writing for. While I might write, "If you are a person who feels everyone has a right to own weapons . . ." or "If you are someone who is willing to ignore economic justice and environmental impact in your shopping decisions . . . ," I wouldn't use "we" because I am not the kind of person I am describing and I want to state that clearly.

If we are writing about tiger beetles, chemical reactions, or soil erosion, we fall easily into a comfortable point of view. However, with humans as our subjects, pronouns are tangled into our deepest values. The choices are not merely a matter of craft but of worldview. Pronouns are about who is included and excluded, about who is in our circle of caring and who is "the other." At the most intense level, pronoun selection is a values clarification task. Pronoun choices concern who we stand with and who we stand against, and, finally, who we choose to call "us."

Because point of view is so complicated, I recommend that you practice working with it. Observe some scenes from each of the vantage points we have discussed—outsider, insider, and connected critic—then write them up, paying full attention to your place in the story. Write a story from the point of view of someone you don't like or respect. Consider the world from their perspective, and note what happens to your heart. Write a narrative with three characters, one of whom causes trouble for the other two. Then write the same story from each of the other character's point of view and see how much wiser you become.

Framing

George Lakoff's book *Don't Think of an Elephant* draws on cognitive science and linguistics to explore how people process information. Lakoff explains that people can only assimilate new facts if these facts fit into the framework they are already using to view the world. If information is discordant with people's overall ways of perceiving and processing, they simply reject it. This phenomenon explains the "I've made up my mind, don't confuse me with the facts" syndrome. Certain facts are so outside readers' frames of reference that they cannot be absorbed by them.

Lakoff argues that persuaders must build bigger frames that connect to more people's experiences. The smaller people's frames, the more lost and confused they will be, and the less they will be able to make good decisions and act adaptively. The bigger the frames, the more realistic people will be.

Our point of view can be defined as the frames through which we view the universe. Over the course of a lifetime, people who grow wiser—and not all of them do—expand their frames of reference and find themselves able to connect to more people and experiences. The best writers enlarge the points of view of their readers. They create overarching metaphors and build bigger frames that allow readers to understand this world more deeply.

One of my favorite examples of point of view and respect for relationship is the introduction to *What God Has Joined Together*, by David Myers and Letha Scanzoni. The authors take on a formidable task:

convincing the faith community to reexamine their attitudes toward gay marriage. Their opening to the reader serves as a model for framing a discussion in a way that opens hearts and minds. I requested permission and the authors graciously agreed to share this excerpt with us.

A Personal Letter to Our Readers

This is a book about marriage. We believe in marriage. We want to see it strengthened. Knowing that strong, healthy, loving relationships are beneficial to the individuals and to any children they might have, we want to see couples flourish. We also believe that society, by supporting marriage, benefits as well.

In other words, we take marriage seriously. We affirm the solemn words of the traditional wedding ceremony in *The Book of Common Prayer* (1892), which asserts that marriage is holy and honorable and should not "be entered into unadvisedly or lightly, but reverently, discreetly, advisedly, soberly, and in the fear of God."

The ceremony tells us that it is a holy estate "into which these two persons present come now to be joined." From this time forward, they will be united in life's closest relationship. When they are asked, "Who is your nearest relative?" they will no longer give the name of mother, father, sister, or brother, but the name of this person, their spouse. They are now kin. They have made a commitment to love, support, comfort, encourage, and respect each other, helping each other to learn and grow and be all they can be—separately and together. They will be there for each other in happy times, in hard times, and in the in-between ordinary everyday moments. They will have a partner in making decisions and sharing in the many pressures and responsibilities of modern life as well as in simply enjoying each other's companionship. In short, they are no longer alone. Ideally, this is what it means to be joined together by God in marriage.

And yet, some who have yearned for such public commitment have been denied it. Over history, some couples have been barred from marriage for reasons of social class, race, or ethnicity. The burning question in our day is whether persons of the same sex should be prevented from sealing their love commitment in socially recognized marriage.

Many people have strong reservations about opening marriage to gays and lesbians. The reasons vary and may be rooted in politics, religion, ideas about gender, misinformation about sexual orientation, fear of societal change, or prejudice and bigotry. There may be other reasons as well. Voices have been raised to suggest that permitting persons of the same sex to marry will destroy the institution. We think not. We believe that opening marriage for gay and lesbian people could actually strengthen the institution for all people. In this book we will show why we believe that.

We not only take marriage seriously, we also take our Christian faith seriously. Among other things, this means that we approach this topic in a spirit of humility, knowing that we "see through a glass darkly," and that none of us has all the answers on this or any other subject. And we speak in a spirit of love, even toward those who vehemently disagree with us. We believe that "since God loved us so much, we also ought to love one another" (John 4:11), and we believe that this means respecting one another, even when we differ in how we interpret Scripture and understand God's working in the world.

The discussion we propose is not about winning arguments, nor is it about some abstract concept. It is about human beings, our brothers and sisters who are loved by God, whether they are heterosexual or homosexual. We bring to the discussion the conclusions we have reached, asking only that our readers be open to listening to and considering what we ourselves have been learning—and continue to learn.

And so we send out this book as an attempt to promote understanding and dialogue in the spirit of Jesus, who not only spoke of the oneness of two persons joined in marriage, but also prayed for oneness in the family of God: "I in them and you in me, that they may become completely one, so that the world may know that you have sent me and have loved them even as you have loved me" (John 17:23).

Myers and Scanzoni know their audience. They start where their readers are, with the core belief that marriage should be encouraged, supported, and strengthened. They write within their readers' frame of reference, quoting *The Book of Common Prayer* and the Bible as evidence for their positions. They employ the language and the values of their readers, and they anticipate and gently refute anticipated arguments. Their tone is respectful, even gentle, and they end with a quote by that great expert of accepting and loving others—Jesus.

Compassion

May this suffering serve to awaken compassion.

—PRAYER TO KWAN YIN

Eugene O'Neill wrote, "Man is born broken. He lives by mending. The Grace of God is glue." Not to be disrespectful to him, or irreverent, but I posit that the mending glue could also be empathy. The word "compassion" means "to suffer with." Reflecting on point of view is an exploration of the nuances of empathy. When we write about others, we move beyond our own identities and try to understand what it feels like to be in someone else's place.

This compassion is built into our choice of topics. When we decide to write about prisoners, dyslexic children, hurricane victims, or sweatshop workers in Mexico, we are becoming advocates. To tell the stories of others is to advocate for them.

With point of view, we are wrestling with our deepest, most existential questions. What deserves our attention? What are we here for? For whom are we responsible? For whom do we feel mercy? What is our purpose?

Point of view is a way to fight what Miguel de Unamuno called "ideocracies," or the tyranny of ideas. The truly bad ideas of humankind—war, religious intolerance, colonialism, racism, the repression of women, communism, fascism, and savage capitalism—have spread because of limited empathy. When zealots bash gays, it is in part because they do not know or understand gay people. Hatred and dogma arise from a certain kind of ignorance about how other people experience their lives.

A man who says "If it's got tits or wheels, it's gonna give me problems" is not well schooled in the points of view of the women in his life, although he certainly may be accurate that women give him trouble. As one of my friends wrote of the liberal bashing she was hearing on talk radio, "They don't know me well enough to hate me this much." Indeed, ideological haters do not know the people they hate. They see them through the thick and distorted glass of their rigid and limited frames.

Empathy shatters ideologies and destroys stereotypes. It is the only thing that works. And teaching point of view is empathy training. Therapists do it when we ask a man to role play his wife or a mother to role play her teenage daughter. A teacher uses point of view when she asks her class to shut their eyes and imagine how the world would seem if they were blind.

When we writers offer readers multiple points of view on the universe, we help them expand their frames of reference. We dissolve prejudices and open hearts and minds. Mastering point of view is a task for a lifetime. Like "growing a soul" and learning to be kind and useful, it is something we work on until we die.

TEN

COOLING DOWN—REVISING

Never think of revising as fixing something that is wrong. That starts you off in a negative frame of mind. Rather think of it as an opportunity to improve something you already love. —MARION DANE BAUER

Writing is demanding work. We learn from trial and error, from analyzing mistakes, and from what Samuel Beckett described as "failing better." I am one of those writers whose work is very bad until it isn't. I plod through dozens of rough drafts, embarrassed by their quality, until, one day, I am not ashamed anymore. This means that I spend about ninety-five percent of my writing time revising. Even after my books are published, I edit them every time I read them at a signing.

Many writers focus on their first drafts, and consider revising dull and painful. Nothing could be further from my experience. To use a gardening analogy, for beginners, planting is generally more fun than weeding or pruning. But for seasoned gardeners, pruning and weeding are creative processes. A few minutes of careful culling can transform a scraggly patch into a bouquet of startling colors. A snip here, a dig and toss there, and an unruly bed bursts into an impressionistic work of art. This is especially true when we are trimming down our favorite writing. Anyone can cut poor writing, but only a serious writer can excise excellent writing that is neither apt nor necessary.

Pause and Rest

When we present emotional, controversial, and complicated material to already harried and stressed readers, we want to make our work brief, eloquent, and inspirational. Writing while in the grip of passion is a fine idea, but revising and sending out our writing should be left to calmer moments. Sometimes, we may feel like scrapping a piece that after a day or two might look more salvageable. More often, when we write in the heat of the moment, we can feel an adrenaline rush that gives us false confidence.

Both time and space give us perspective, and allow us to reflect on how others might react to our writing. A vacation, or a week of other projects, will enable us to see our work with clearer eyes. Even when we are past a deadline, we should pause for lunch or a walk around the block. Then we can return clearheaded to read our piece one last time. Eventually, we learn to resist the "I just want to get this over with" impulse.

Pausing in our work can be compared to allowing fields to lie fallow. Our thinking is underground, but still critical and creative. A good rule of thumb is, The longer the piece, the longer the wait should be. There are exceptions, of course. Some great writing was done in the heat of the moment. I think of Jon Krakauer's *Into Thin Air*. The author felt he had rushed it, and that he had been too close to the events on Mount Everest to do them justice. However, readers disagreed, and instead responded to his intense feelings about the expeditions. At a time when many readers were curious to know what happened, Krakauer could provide an account by a participant. We could almost feel the wind and snow as we turned the pages.

Read Your Work Aloud

One summer, when my daughter Sara was home from college, I read her my manuscript for *Another Country*. As I read, I found myself embarrassed by some sections and bored by others. I caught myself sounding pretentious or out of touch. I heard the clunky, the hyperbolic, the repetitious, and the gassy opining. I noticed what caused Sara to space out and what caused her to attend carefully.

Writers benefit from reading aloud to people who do not think as we do. We can see the psychological effects of our work on them; not only can we hear their opinions after we read, but we'll also have a sense for what they may not be able to tell us. We also can notice what their physical reactions are to our work. Do they tense up, frown, or nod in agreement as we read?

If readers have strong negative reactions, we do not have to change our writing, but we will have more information about our effects on others. It is too bad that most of us don't have access to a speaker's corner, with its instant visual and verbal feedback. However, we can read to our writers' workshops, book clubs, church groups, or PTA meetings.

Brevity

The Buddhist rule for right speech—"Speak only words that are kind, useful, and true"—is a good rule for writers as well. As we revise, we can also ask, Am I economical in the service of great ideas? Am I in relationship to my readers and connecting them to something important?

Our goal as writers is to convey to readers the greatest meaning with the most precise images and the fewest words. With many kinds of writing, such as newsletters, book reviews, or op-ed pieces, we don't have much space in which to explain complex issues. Readers scan hundreds of messages that compete for their limited time. They won't bother reading wordy, overwritten material.

Most of us learned to write by doing school assignments, with length a primary requirement. We tried to fill up the most paper possible. We must jettison that habit. We want to avoid trendy and trite phrases, and to be cautious about words that offer readers merely empty padding. We do not need vague such modifiers as "very," "kind of," "in general," and especially "I think." The entire piece is what we think. We want to erase "Tom Swiftlys," so named because of all the dopey adverbs in the Swift books: "He hung onto the cliff heroically," or "Hungrily, he made his way to the dinner table."

My personal pet peeve is the misuse of the word "frankly" to establish a pretend intimacy. If you use "frankly" or "to be frank," please say something frank. "Frank" means not only are you speaking honestly, you are risking that your listeners will dislike what you say or judge you harshly. Do not say, "Frankly, I have always wanted to raft the Colorado River." Where is the risk-taking self-disclosure in that sentence? A frank statement could be something like this: "Frankly, I myself have committed all of the seven deadly sins."

Use Your Audience to Help You Focus

A Mormon friend once told me that almost no one is converted by the young missionaries sent by the church all over the world. Rather naively, I asked her, "Then why does the church send thousands of young men abroad?" She smiled, and said, "After two years of trying to convince others, the missionaries become true believers and never leave the church. This is our way of keeping our young people in the faith." Unlike effective change writers, these missionaries converted no one. But they did become clearer about and more deeply committed to their own messages. Audience was a focusing force.

When we write, we dive down into an intensely individual process, but when we revise we surface to think about our readers. We ask, Who are we trying to influence, and what do we want our influence to be? As we picture our audience, we organize and edit our thoughts. When we write for people who think as we do, we want to keep them focused and committed to our mutual goals. When we write for readers who are neither true believers nor total naysayers, we are hoping to open minds and encourage fresh thinking. Depending on our audience, we will revise our writing in certain ways.

PREACHING TO THE CHOIR

The truth is, most preaching *is* to the choir. Choirs produce almost all the important social action in our world. The people most likely to read us are people who think like we do. And readers generally seek reinforcement of their beliefs, not arguments or challenges. When writing for compatriots, we hope to energize and sustain them. We want to deliver new thoughts and information to them, strengthen their beliefs, and mobilize them to action. Often, we will cite common history and heroes, and employ shared, meaning-laden metaphors. This kind of "to the barricades" writing enjoins communities of believers to make things happen.

WRITING FOR THE UNCONVINCED

Sometimes, the goal is to win over people who do not think as we do. This category may well include family, friends, and most of the people we know. In fact, unless we are writing for a targeted, narrow group, we can assume that people have experienced their lives in ways that have led them to conclusions quite different from our own.

Recently, on a writers' camping trip, one of our members shocked us by confessing that she was a Republican. She was from a military family, and was married to a deeply conservative man. She had camped with us for years before she trusted us enough to out herself as a conservative. Before the Iraq war, she had been invited many times to read something at Poets Against the War rallies. She said ruefully, "It never occurred to anyone that a poet might support the war."

Writing for the unconvinced, we want to be respectful and enticing. We need to invite them into our world and establish commonality. All humans yearn to be happy and free of suffering. All want to be useful, safe, loved, and understood. Furthermore, almost all of us wish all people could be safe, well educated, healthy, and free. We just have very different ideas about how to achieve these goals.

To avoid resistance, it's best to focus on common needs and problems. Readers should be nodding their heads in agreement, and, later, when we discuss solutions, we want them thinking, I want to follow these suggestions and help out.

It can be counterproductive to identify ourselves as a member of an established group. Words such as "liberal," "feminist," "pro-life," or "evangelical" push certain buttons in many people. We want readers to think about our ideas, not fly off into their own trance of a thousand voices.

I am proud to call myself an environmentalist. However, many Americans—and certainly a majority of those who actually make their living farming, logging, and fishing—dislike environmentalists. With these groups, I might want to discuss my ideas without using a word that calls forth such an intense reaction. For the most part, people who label environmentalists "tree huggers" do not dislike parks where they can enjoy the outdoors with their families. I can appeal to our mutual love of these things. They also like fresh air, clean water, and green vistas. They too enjoy watching birds and animals, and want their children to grow up with some connection to nature. They would agree with the general idea that we need to protect the earth for future generations, including their own great-great-grandchildren. And, most likely, they have happy memories of times out of doors. As I generate this list, I can envision many ways into a discussion of environmental issues without using any labels.

On the other hand, sometimes I want to use our cultural labels. I think that if I, a feminist and a human rights activist, do not claim these words, then I leave their use to those who use them to mock and denigrate. I do not want others to define me, and I resist ceding my language to those who dislike my causes. I want to remind people that decent people identify themselves proudly with certain causes. So the question of labels is a complex one, as is almost every other question that involves persuasion. The question is, Do we risk relationship to promote our causes? The answer: It depends.

Readers

I share all my work with friends or family before I present it, dressed up in its Sunday best for all to see. My friend Pam generally reads my first messy manuscript. After she reads it, I buy her lunch, and we talk through the ideas in the book. She is kind and optimistic, and she points me toward the most promising material. She carefully shows me simplistic, confusing, or contradictory passages. Still, she always ends these feedback sessions with: "I can't wait to read this book when it's finished."

The trick for finding honest readers is being appreciative of their time, and respectful and relaxed about their criticisms. Friends and associates will not want to be negative about our work, but if we show them we can handle criticism gracefully and gratefully they will speak forthrightly. Many writers pay for this service, and that's fine too. Whoever we work with is giving us the gift of their time and attention.

I often send out as many as fifteen manuscripts in progress to a diverse group of readers: some English majors, a journalist, an academic or two with relevant expertise, and a host of ordinary Joes and Joettes. I also want to know what my cousins, my favorite convenience store clerk, and my neighbors think.

Especially with dozens of critics looking at a manuscript, feedback can be intense and difficult to decipher. Sometimes, readers have opposite reactions. "Lose this section" can refer to something that another reader labeled "My favorite part." In the end, I make my own judgments.

Here is a copy of the letter I sent with my manuscript of *The Middle of Everywhere*. It gives you a sense of my expectations of them.

Dear readers,

Let me begin by thanking you for your time. I know every one of you is busy, and I am grateful for the gift of your lovely precious hours. Please be honest. I much prefer to hear criticism from my friends, while I can still correct problems, than to read criticism in reviews. You are doing me a great favor by telling me the truth. Don't hold back.

Please help me cull any tired language, repetition, or psychologese. Help me eliminate awkward phrases, puffed-up language, and ten-dollar words. I can be preachy, and I want you to tell me when I sound shrill or soap-boxy.

Let me know where you doubt my credibility, find yourself arguing with me, or think my language is sloppy. Please keep these questions in mind:

What do you find fresh and intriguing?

Where do you find yourself drifting?

What can be cut? Include whole essays if you think they are dull or repetitive.

What is trite, dull, academic, or too abstract?

Where do you want more stories?

What do you think of the order of essays? Any awkward segues?

What did I leave out that you would like to know? Again, include whole essay ideas if you want.

Finally, how can I make it better in the broadest sense?

This is a lot of work for you. I deeply appreciate your help. I will send you a book when it is out. Please, share *all* your thoughts. Thanks, dear friends.

The Perfect Title

With titles, we set up expectations and deliver information about the content and themes of our work. Good titles are also how we find readers. There is a fine line between catchy and cutesy, however. While titles with multiple meanings can be powerful, easy puns grow tiresome. There are too many articles entitled "Family Matters," "Sage Advice for Cooking Thyme," and "Fiddling Around." The following book titles grabbed my attention: *The Americanization of Sex* (Edwin Schur), *Full Catastrophe Living* (Jon Kabat-Zinn), *Fast Food Nation* (Eric Schlosser), *The Global Soul* (Pico Iyer), *A Distant Mirror* (Barbara Tuchman), *Jihad vs. McWorld* (Benjamin Barber), *Silicon Snake Oil* (Clifford Stoll), and *Born to Buy* (Juliet Schor). These titles promise a new way of understanding the world and piqued my curiosity about what the authors had to say.

As we grow into our topics, we may change titles many times. The best titles have a way of hitting us on the head as they fall from the sky. Titles both can be epiphanies, and can induce epiphanies in others. A great title will elicit an "Aha" from us when we discover it, and later from our readers when they make the connection between the title and the meaning of our work. With a title, shoot for perfect, go for broke.

Beginnings and Endings

> Nobody reads a book to get to the middle.
>
> —MICKEY SPILLANE

We want bang-up beginnings and endings for paragraphs, sections, and chapters, and for the whole work. Great beginnings connect with something deep inside us and make us want to read on. Great endings strike us as slightly surprising yet inevitable. Perfect endings strike us as just what we wanted, but we didn't know it.

Let me warn you about endings. In many books and articles, writers run out of gas before they finish the race. They pour all their energy into the first part, then, suddenly, sputter to a stop. You may have noted that toward the end of a book, writing is often wordier and sloppier. That is because writers, every time we correct a manuscript, tend to read it from beginning to end, so that the first part is read many more times than the later part. Watch out for that. Vary the ways you end a piece.

Finally, to leave you even more burdened with suggestions, don't forget the middle, where books often sag. In short, every part of the book is difficult.

Think About Readers One More Time

We are trying to woo a very hard-to-win date. Often, our favorite writing just won't do and has to go. People who think the same as we do might be impressed by our most impassioned passages, but others will find them too incendiary. Our quest is to be persuasive without watering down our core ideas. That takes lots of experimentation and effort.

We want to scan our writing for whiffs of condescension, and ask ourselves, Is it clear and reader-friendly? Where are readers likely to resist? Am I accidentally using code or hot-button words that carry more meanings than I intend? (For example, while the phrase "government spending" is not upsetting to some, with others it can cause a visceral reaction.

In *Reviving Ophelia,* I was careful to never compare the suffering of girls to that of boys. First of all, social scientists cannot prove that the one group suffers more than the other. Second, I had noticed that when people suggested that girls had more trouble than boys, they found themselves immediately in an argument. So I steered clear. I wrote that I had a son and a daughter whom I loved equally, and that I was opining about girls not because I felt girls were needier or more valuable than boys but because I had been a girl once and because I was a therapist for girls.

In my book, I tried not to pick on anyone. I selected a diverse group of girls, family types, and problems. I was careful to use PG-rated language. Some of my favorite writers use swear words. That does not offend me, but it does offend others, and it limits their audience. Many college campuses will not allow books that have the F-word.

Still, no matter how careful we are, as change agents we will have our detractors. We must be prepared for controversy. When vested interests challenge our authority, we want our facts and logic to be in order. However, in our writing, and when defending our writing, we need not know everything. We only need to be honest about what we know and what we do not know.

Crying Uncle

By the time I call a manuscript finished, I have revised it forty to fifty times. Toward the end, I feel as if the book is my significant other. Especially in the last months, I think more about the writing than I do about real people. How do I know when to stop?

One writer said he stops when he spends all morning taking out a comma and all afternoon putting it back in. I stop when I become blind to the manuscript, when I have more or less memorized it, and when my attempts to improve it make it worse.

Toward the end of revising, I will often wake up in the middle of the night, visualizing, in red ink, a specific sentence from my manuscript. I can see the entire page, and I know the page number. Red means I need to rewrite that sentence. When I wake up like that, I know I am approaching the end. I stop obsessing about the book, and wonder if my husband would like to go for a walk.

Defining Success

Success is not a numbers game. Quality is not quantity. Certain books have sold relatively few copies, but they have aided the progress of humankind. Editorials in small newspapers have swung elections. Scholarly articles that originally were ignored have changed the course of history. Most of us will not influence world history. However, we succeed if we move things along by just one of Baldwin's millimeters.

Life is much too extraordinary to be completely captured in

words, even beautiful and carefully selected ones. We must train ourselves to be compassionate about our failures. It is not our fault that
we don't have IQs of 300, that we live near a noisy Amtrak line, or
that our mother just had hip replacement surgery and needs our attention. We all work within constraints that define us, hinder us, and
teach us what we need to know.

Success means we have done our best. We have not squandered
our gifts or ignored our responsibilities. We have given our time and
talents to help others. We have used our freedom to free someone
else. Success is not fame or awards; it is having our ideas discussed by
other people.

Our work is about something much bigger and more important
than we are. In the long run, success means we secure a place in the
centuries-old pantheon of people who care about ideas. We find our
chair at the tired, tormented yet joyous old table of humankind. If
we are really lucky, we even manage to make room for others there.

With success, the muse whispers in our ears, "Well done, my good
and faithful servant."

PART THREE

Calls to Action

ELEVEN

LETTERS

The first job of the citizen is to keep your mouth open.

—GÜNTER GRASS

One of the chief privileges of man is to speak up for the universe.   —NORMAN MACLEAN

We have it in our power to begin the world again.

—THOMAS PAINE

Spring Creek Prairie vs. Commercial Motocross

Spring Creek Prairie, just outside of Lincoln, Nebraska, is what scientists call a signature landscape, representative of the original ecosystem of our central plains. It is 626 acres of never-plowed, tall-grass prairie, which contains wetlands, natural springs, creeks, ponds, and indigenous woodlands—bur oak, cottonwood, and hackberry trees. More than 192 species of birds and more than 350 species of plants have been identified at Spring Creek Prairie. The prairie also includes Native American relics dating back thousands of years, and wagon ruts from the Nebraska City–Fort Kearney cutoff to the Oregon Trail.

Audubon Nebraska purchased Spring Creek Prairie in 1998. My husband and I love to visit it, walking often through its tall red grasses, touching its Oregon Trail ruts, and, in the spring, observing a lek where prairie chickens dance. We know where its arrowheads were discovered, and where its coneflowers and nodding ladies tresses grow. We have picnicked by its buffalo wallows, where, centuries ago, buffalo rubbed their itchy backs on large rocks, and, over time, formed moats around these rocks.

In January 2004, the director of Audubon Nebraska called us to say that the prairie was in danger. A private landowner planned to build a commercial motocross racetrack on nearby land. The noise alone would destroy the bird-watching on the prairie; visitors wouldn't be able to hear the birds. The birds also might be frightened and leave the area, but even if they stayed they might be unable to hear one another and mate. The director asked us to help in the campaign to save the prairie.

My first reaction was, "Oh please, not now." I was in the middle of my last quiet month for writing this book. Beginning in February, I had a slate of interviews, speaking engagements, and trips around the country. I viewed this crisis as an interruption of other serious projects. However, as often happens in my life, what seems like an unwelcome intrusion turns out to be an important lesson.

I thought I knew a great deal about persuasive writing already. However, when tested in the messy lab of political reality, what I thought I knew turned out to be wrong. Here is my letter to the five-member county board that made the decision about zoning for or against the motocross. I began with a literary quote:

"There is a timeless wisdom that survives failed economies and wars. It is a nameless wisdom stressed by all people. It is understanding how to live a decent life, how to behave properly towards other people and the land" (Barry Lopez).

I am a writer, a member of Audubon Nebraska, and a friend of Spring Creek Prairie. I walk on it in all the seasons. I dig up musk thistles on hot Saturday mornings. I attend its festivals and its sunsets. I visit it alone when I need stillness and solitude.

Next summer I plan to take my two-year-old granddaughter to Spring Creek Prairie. As she grows up, I hope it will be part of the landscape of her life.

Since I have been an established writer, I have shown our prairie to many visitors including, on separate occasions, a *New York Times* reporter and the head of European Clinical Psychology. As we walked, both of them became silent and their breathing slowed down. The reporter said, "I know why you live in Nebraska." Enjoying an August sunset, the psychologist from Scotland said, "This was worth the trip." I thought he meant from my house, but he added, "From Scotland, I mean."

My writers' group, all nationally published, spends time together on the prairie. We call ourselves Prairie Trout, and regard, as sources of our inspiration, the birds, the big sky, the silence, and the grasses in all their different colors.

After Bob Dylan wrote "Blowin' in the Wind," someone asked him what he meant by that phrase. He said, "If you have ever listened to the wind blow, you know what I mean. If you haven't, I can't explain it."

I feel that way today. Who can measure the effects of birdsong, the breeze blowing through tall grasses, or the beauty of prairie orchids? These things cannot be discussed in terms of money. They are of a different order of value. They keep us human, grounded, and sane. They give us joy, peace, and a connection to something much larger and older than ourselves.

This proposed motocross track would deeply interfere with our prairie and substantially diminish its ability to give us its gifts. I cannot imagine the reactions of my friends from around the world to the roar of motorbikes on our beautiful, pristine prairie. I don't want to ponder what my granddaughter will miss if this permit is approved. In our noisy, machine-filled world, there are few magic patches left. Spring Creek Prairie is one of them. I urge you to visit it and to protect it for yourselves, for all of us, and for our children and their children.

Thank you.

I was quite proud of this letter, and my friend Ray Stevens, the chair of the county board, later told me that it was the most literate, lovely letter the board received. However, as the hearings unfurled, I realized with chagrin that my letter was not effective. My eloquent plea angered one of the board members whose vote was critical. I suspect he thought I was showing off. Quoting Bob Dylan, a symbol of the radical sixties, was probably a big mistake. Even my literary quotation was naive: Most people do not know who Barry Lopez is. Some of us like quotes, but others may react to them by feeling put off or defensive. My mention of my writing career, which I had hoped would give me authority, in retrospect, looks a bit braggy and pompous.

My letter about prairie grasses and the sound of the wind was preaching to the converted. There was not one word in my letter that connected me with the board members, or granted any legitimacy to the other side. In fact, I was a polarizing figure. In the end, the people who could connect to both sides of the issue were the ones who saved the day.

Here's an example of a more effective letter, written by my friend, Karen Shoemaker:

Dear County Board Member,

I am writing in regard to the special permit request for a motocross track north of Spring Creek Prairie. I'd like to start by admitting that I would not want your job as commissioner, but I am grateful to women and men like you who are willing to do this work. I appreciate that the task before you is not easy and I know you are all good people trying to make the best decision possible.

Motocross is a fun sport, and it deserves the time and space the developers are hoping to give it. However, I submit there are more appropriate locations for it than next to a serene and beautiful prairie. My husband runs a truck stop out on West O Street. When I told him about my sadness about the potential harm that may soon befall the prairie, he commented that there is so much land right out near his business that would be perfect for a motocross track. The land south of West O Street along the railroad track is hilly and undeveloped. It's close to the city, and the noise created by racing would be negligible compared to the railroad and airport noise already a part of the area's atmosphere. As an added bonus, many of the neighbors would be delighted to see motocross fans and participants frequenting the area.

In the public hearing on February 24, it was claimed by proponents for the track that they cannot find a better place for their chosen business. I don't believe that is true, and I hope you don't either. Please tell the proponents for the track to keep looking until they find a place that is suited for, not just expedient to, their needs.

I have two children: a sixteen-year-old boy who would love to see a motocross track in Lancaster County, and a ten-year-old girl who loves to walk the trails and study the wildlife on the prairie. This is only one example of the differences between them that I negotiate on a daily basis. I do my best to ensure that the needs and wants of one do not override the needs and wants of the other. It's not an easy task, as I'm sure you can appreciate. Sometimes, the solution is a matter of redirecting. I believe that's the solution to the issue before the commission at this time. Direct the motocross proponents to find a place that will not harm our natural treasures, please.

I know you have heard from others about the importance of the prairie as an educational center, research facility, and wildlife sanctuary. I agree with all those points, but for me this issue is also very personal. Let me explain. A friend and I were walking on Spring Creek Prairie on the morning of September 11, 2001. It was a blue-sky-beautiful morning filled with birdsong and the whisper of a breeze through the prairie grasses. A man was moving cattle off to the south of the trail we walked, and we heard him call "Here, Boss" to the cattle. Have you ever heard a man call his cattle with that phrase? I hadn't heard it since my grandfather sold his cattle nearly thirty-five years ago. In that moment, on that prairie, I felt entirely connected to the history of my family, to my state, even to this world. I was completely happy standing there on that spot, just listening. When our walk ended, we came back to the news that our nation had been attacked. I have returned to the prairie dozens of times since that morning for the solace only the prairie can give. I beg of you, do not let anyone destroy that peace.

Karen Shoemaker

Karen's letter is a masterpiece of connection. She employs a respectful and affectionate tone. She is empathic about the complexity of the issues, yet hopeful too. Her letter skillfully connects her to almost all groups involved in the dispute: teenage boys who love excitement, motocross fans, businesspeople, nature lovers, and environmentalists. Her likening of the board's predicament to her own as a mother is artful. She ends with a heartwarming story designed to evoke memories in board members of their own rural backgrounds, something almost all middle-aged Nebraskans share. Finally, her repeated use of "please" is polite and yet urgent, especially when she uses it to end her letter. Karen's letter made it very difficult for members to discount her message.

The county board received hundreds of letters about Spring Creek Prairie and the motocross. Ray Stevens told me that the most influential letters were from scientists or revered people from the community. Emotional arguments or those containing scurrilous remarks were heavily discounted. Nearby property owners who fought to protect property values did not persuade, but neighbors' quality-of-life arguments did. Two board members owned acreages and they could appreciate the value of silence.

The sheer numbers of letters in support of the prairie helped, as did letters with convincing arguments about the public good. For example, the letter from Audubon Nebraska showed that they had spent millions of dollars investing in the land and education center for the prairie, and that it would cost taxpayers $350,000 to pave the county road for motocross.

Letters from children were surprisingly effective. The board members were parents and grandparents who valued education and access to the natural world. Ray told me about one letter from a girl in which she drew a picture of birds with noise-reducing earmuffs on. She asked plaintively, "Who is going to buy all the birds earmuffs?"

In the end, the protectors of Spring Creek Prairie eked out a victory. The board had two members strongly opposed to the motocross and two for it. The fifth member, sitting on the fence, eventually decided to vote against it. The board agreed with the point Karen made, that there was a need for a motocross facility but not in this place.

Before the good news was announced, prairie supporters suffered major stress, frustration, and despair. However, we also learned a great deal about effective lobbying. Those of us who mobilized to save the prairie grew clearer and stronger about our purpose. We shared a moral assignment that gave us courage to keep going when we were maligned and disheartened. We used this crisis to introduce new people to the beauty and importance of Spring Creek Prairie, and we increased awareness of issues around land use in our county.

After our victory, we held a healing ceremony on the prairie. The staff, my husband and I, and a historian who studied the Oregon Trail ruts met on a late afternoon in March. All week the weather had been gray, drizzly, and windy; but around 4 P.M. the winds died down and the sun came out. The clouds rapidly skidded east.

We hiked for a while through the tall yellow grass. On the dam, we passed tracks of beaver, skunk, coyote, rabbit, and fox. A muskrat swam in the pond. We heard the first spring peepers, and meadowlarks, a bird that lives only in beautiful places. As we searched for the right place to hold our ceremony, one staff member said, "Anyplace on the prairie is the right place."

Three prairie chickens flew up in front of us as we climbed a gentle hill covered with big bluestem grass. We all agreed that they had shown us our spot. We lay on the hillside in the deep yellow grass, which in the sun felt like a warm hemp mat.

We looked at the sky, felt the breeze on our winter-pale faces, and breathed in the smells of sage, dirt, and new green growth. We read poems by Wendell Berry and Walt Whitman, and talked about the experience of fighting to save the prairie. Jim played guitar and sang Stephen Foster's "Hard Times Come Again No More." We all sang Woody Guthrie's "This Land Is Your Land." Finally, we just lay side by side and listened to the wind blow across grasses that Willa Cather once described as "a great red inland sea."

The sun dropped low in the west, the pond shimmered silvery blue. Mallards and snow geese flew over us. We finished by reading a letter to activists by Edward Abbey, that most fiercely passionate of environmentalists. Then we hugged each other and walked to our cars, and back to our lives in the world of cell phones and machines.

Driving home, I thought of this small group of people who loved the prairie. Much of the work in any movement depends on hard-core believers who will work ten hours a day, week after week and year after year, to protect what they love. These "worker bees" are in for the long haul. With this chapter, I wanted to write something that could help passionate advocates become convincing spokespeople for their beloved causes. Being right is not enough. Facts and evidence are not enough. Eloquence is not enough. Building a relationship to the people we wish to persuade is what often does the trick. And, when we win, we should celebrate.

Talking to public servants was an interesting way to research questions of influence. Nebraska senator DiAnna Schimek said that letters help politicians make decisions concerning issues about which they are conflicted or uncertain. Mail has limited impact on decisions when politicians already hold firm opinions.

She gave an example from her current work. The legislature is debating a bill on taxation of retired military personnel's pensions. It is a complex piece of legislation with ramifications for business, the state's tax base, and fairness to other retired people. Schimek has been carefully reading her mail on this issue for six months, and letters will influence her vote. She has still not decided her position.

On the other hand, Senator Schimek introduced a bill three years in a row that restores the vote to felons who have served their time. Letters have not influenced her position, except to make it stronger. She has received many letters from prisoners who tell her how important it is for them to be able to participate as citizens in our democracy.

She said the most compelling letters were handwritten and heartfelt. The personal stories of people who would be affected by this bill had great persuasive power. Testimony at the public hearing from prisoners and ex-felons, their friends and families and advocacy groups, also deeply influenced the senators. In our quite conservative state, the majority of senators voted for this bill, and later even voted to override the governor's veto to make it law.

All the government officials I spoke with emphasized the importance of brevity in letters. Many said they pay much more attention to their own constituents than to outsiders. They also pay attention to people they know. Form letters or postcards are tossed. Self-righteous or angry letters tend to be ignored. I saw examples of some doozies. One letter began, "Read the enclosed and get the hell out of our lives. It was a sure thing that ilk like you would be trying to fight for your miserable wannabe political life but you are fighting a losing battle. . . ." Tossed.

Politicians pay attention to personal stories about the impact policies have on voters. They also are influenced by letters of appreciation. Many politicos said they choke up when they receive thank-you notes. I inferred from this that gratitude is in short supply for people in public life.

In spite of the fact that I was talking about letters, many politicians brought up the importance of face-to-face meetings. Lincoln City Council member Terry Werner recommended that if an issue is really an important one, ask for a meeting to follow up on your letter. All politics is local. It's relatively easy to sway people over coffee and doughnuts.

Elements of a Persuasive Letter

In the beginning and all the way through your letter, respect your reader, find some common ground, and, as much as you can, keep to what you hold in common. Empathize with the person you are writing to: "I know being mayor is a thankless job," or "The problems around light rail transit are complex and fraught with political and financial problems, and I appreciate that you are working on solutions." Or "Even though we differ on how to meet our goals, we can agree that we do want affordable health care for everyone in our community."

Make sure that you know the point of your letter, and that your reader can also discern it. Exactly what do you want to achieve by writing this letter? What actions do you hope the recipient will take? A surprising number of advocacy letters or letters to the editor leave readers wondering, What is this person trying to say? Or, Huh? What does he want?

Keep your language simple. Avoid ten-dollar words, academic language, or acronyms. Be straightforward. A reader, especially one who doesn't know you, is unlikely to know when you are joking or being sarcastic. Robert Frost did quite well with simple words and you can too. Mental clarity combined with brevity can be extremely powerful.

Positive predictions have a way of becoming self-fulfilling prophecies. Hope is infectious. It is better to write "Let us create humane learning environments for all prisoners in our state" than "Our prison system is a horrible mess." And include a statement of optimism: "These are tough problems to solve, but I am certain that if we work hard together and support each other on this project we will be successful."

When I must write a letter that includes criticism, I use what I call "the sandwich method." I begin by stating what I like and value, then I sandwich in problems and controversial issues that must be addressed. Then I return to my original regard for the other person, my optimism, and my sincere desire to make things work for both of us. It is hard for anyone to resist a letter filled with kindness, compliments, generosity, and hope.

Letters to change the world often end with a suggestion for action. Sometimes, these are concrete suggestions, such as "Let's meet next week and discuss these issues" or "I invite you to come with me to the prairie so that you can see its magnificence for yourself." Here is an e-mail from a fifteen-year-old named Natalia Ledford. I like its clarity, authenticity, and heart. Natalia writes in a way that connects with me, and she issues a strong call to action.

Hello! It's Natalia, and I want to invite you to come see the film *Invisible Children*. We saw it at our school and it inspired us. Now we are trying to raise awareness/funds for it and are inviting you to come see the film on the 12th of July. (Admission is free.)

For those who have not already seen or heard about the film: It is about the war going on right now in Uganda with the LRA. (The LRA is the Lord's Resistance Army, a rebel army that is trying to overthrow the government.) It's unlike any other war because the soldiers are not volunteers but children who have been kidnapped and forced to fight. The LRA brainwashes them with violence and gore from the second they arrive at the training camps and the LRA also forces them to kill other children and witness the killings of children. The LRA targets children who are between the ages of 5 to 14; big enough to hold a gun, but young enough that their minds are still very moldable. The abducted children grow up violent and mentally unstable.

This is a moral outrage. Even children who have not been abducted suffer painful lives because of this conflict between the LRA and the government. They are too afraid to sleep at home because they could be kidnapped. Instead, they sleep in town at night. Not in hotels, but on the streets under verandas, at bus stops and in crowded parking lots or hospital hallways. These places are not clean or supervised by adults. They are not fit to house all of these kids, but the poor children have no choice. The situation in Uganda has been described as "one of the most dire humanitarian crises in the world" by the BBC. It's unacceptable, yet is being largely ignored by the international community. It must be brought to everyone's attention.

My sister and I were just touched by the film when we saw it at Lincoln High and now really want to expose this tragic story to more people to raise money and awareness about the issue. We will show the film on Tuesday, July 12th, 6:00 p.m., at Friedens Lutheran Church. Admission is free. Please come and bring as many people as possible. There will be an opportunity to donate money to help.

If you can't make it on Tuesday, check out the website: www .invisiblechildren.com. Feel free to forward this e-mail to anyone. Thank you, I hope to see you there.

Sincerely, Natalia Ledford

Many people attended the church event and participated in an auction for a quilt donated by Natalia and Hannah's grandmother. Money rolled in that night, and they are still receiving donations. The sisters' story, and the story of *Invisible Children,* were featured in a *Lincoln Journal Star* newspaper article. In the article, the sisters suggested that readers rent the DVD and host viewing parties in their living rooms. Because of their commitment and energy level, these girls helped many people in Lincoln expand their circle of caring to include children in Uganda. They changed things by a Baldwin millimeter.

TWELVE

SPEECHES

> The artist tells the audience, at the risk of their displeasure, the secrets of their own hearts.　——ROBIN COLLINGWOOD

> Speeches at conventions compress the largest possible amount of words into the smallest amount of thought.
> ——WINSTON CHURCHILL

> A good sermon is one side of a passionate conversation.
> ——MARILYN ROBINSON

> In the end we will conserve only what we love. We will love only what we understand. We will understand only what we are taught.　——BABA DIOUM

When we speak, we enter into a short-term relationship with our listeners. We agree to spend time together, and the audience grants us permission to influence them. We give them our best thinking. There are three aspects of a speech: content, delivery, and presence. None of these aspects can stand alone. Without a strong delivery and a compelling presence, a speaker, no matter what the content, will not inspire. Skillful presenters hold their audiences' attention. People listening experience a strong personal connection to the speaker and to one another. They should feel transformed, a part of something world changing.

Skillful speeches say to all: You are welcome here. They give writers the opportunity to build community, promulgate ideas, and broaden our audience. Speeches are proximal events; we can see, hear, and even touch our audiences, and vice versa. As speakers, we can test-drive new ideas, and hone them as they elicit reactions from others. After I deliver a speech, I dash off a line-by-line critique of what worked and what did not. I note where the audience members seemed to stray, or where they laughed, or held their breath in anticipation. I review the questions and comments of worthy opponents so that I can consider their points of view. If I give the same speech a second time, I go over my notes so I can do an experience-based edit of it.

All kinds of groups and organizations invite speakers. You can find an audience for your writing by volunteering to speak in front of classes, at churches, and at community forums, rallies, ceremonies, and meetings. Prepare thoroughly, and show up alert and ready for lively interactions. I spend as much time composing a speech as I do writing an article for publication. I free-write my thoughts, then organize and develop them. I do my research, then carefully balance facts, stories, and logical argument. Finally, I reread and edit.

Preparing this way will alleviate anxiety. When your speech is over, you will feel proud of yourself for putting your ideas on the line where they can make a difference.

All kinds of change agents utilize speeches to accomplish their missions. An urban planner may convene a community forum to discuss zoning and the need for a comprehensive urban plan. A minister may talk about the poverty he witnessed on a missions trip and what can be done about it. A builder may lead training sessions on solar power or straw bale construction. A resident in a cohousing program may describe her home to people who know nothing about the cohousing movement. A lawyer may lecture on mediation skills, or a psychologist may teach deep-listening techniques. A teacher may speak about the effects on her classroom of the No Child Left Behind Act. A scientist might advocate a nationwide effort to discuss how politics is influencing research funding. Or the head of a non-profit may share his agency's mission and ask for support.

Sometimes, the most eloquent speakers are those who simply speak about their own experiences. One good example can be worth a dozen theories. Once, I spoke at an Ophelia Project in Tampa. My speech was well received, but it was followed by a speech that brought down the house and filled the coffers of the organization. A young girl from a difficult background, speaking for the first time in public, told about what the project had meant to her life. Her heartfelt eloquence was inspiring.

While effective speakers can benefit any cause, boring, obnoxious, or ill-informed ones can do great harm. For most people, speaking is not an innate gift but rather a learned skill. If you speak in public, you will want to educate yourself on how to do it well. Observe other speakers. Learn to use a microphone. Start with a small audience and work your way up. And practice, practice, practice.

Think about your audience. What are their needs, worries, beliefs, goals, and dreams? Approach them as a sincere individual eager to share what you deeply believe. Have your material organized. Practice pacing. Think about flow and dynamics. Tell stories that support your points. And tell the truth as you see it, and tell it straight. The audience will sense your passion, and that you are informed and prepared, and respond accordingly.

Preparation and Content

The secret to speaking with confidence is having faith in your ideas and in your writing. Confidence comes from preparation. The hardest-working speakers, like the hardest-working dancers or actors, make their work look effortless. I groan when I hear a speaker begin a talk by saying, "I haven't prepared any remarks . . ." Most speakers who do not put effort into their writing are rambling and ineffective, talking long and saying little.

Good speeches require advance research about your audience. To get a sense for recent and relevant events in the community you are going to address, read local papers or talk to event organizers. You may learn of the suicide of a high school student, or the closure of a factory that is the town's major employer, or of the state championship of the basketball team, or of the swearing in of a new mayor. Sometimes, a local hero or magnificent project provides you with an opportunity to praise the community, and to connect your own ideas with theirs.

Psychologists know that first and last impressions are critical in forming an opinion. Opening remarks are by no means incidental. Begin by making eye contact and smiling. Thank people for coming, and praise the people or place you are visiting: "I have great respect for librarians," or "I've never been to Missoula before and it's amazing," or "I have long respected this group's work, and I feel I am with kindred spirits." Sincere praise is a guaranteed pathway into the hearts of your audience.

I try not to waste any opportunities for "teachable moments." I praise clean water, green space, well-educated children, and good community services for elders. In Boston, I almost always mention the beautiful old sycamores along the Charles River. When I am by the ocean, I say how magical it is to someone like myself who grew up in the middle of the country. By praising nature, I hope to encourage others to look for pleasure in nature too.

Depending on our audiences, we may present ourselves differently. We must be in relationship with our audiences in order to influence them. People listen best to those with whom they identify, so we want to share what we have in common. I am a wife, a mother, a grandmother, a bird-watcher, a reader, a therapist, an academic, a writer, a teacher, an Ozark daughter, and a Nebraskan from a working-class background. When I seek to bond with new people, one of those identities will be right.

When I was in Okinawa and Tokyo making speeches for the United States Army, I opened my talks to the troops with stories of my father. He had fought in the South Pacific during World War II, and was stationed in both Okinawa and Tokyo. I mentioned that when he left his small town in the Ozarks, his mother and sisters cried at the station. As my aunt Henrietta later told me, "Nobody in our family had gone that far from home before." Like my father had been, this audience was mostly poor, rural, and from the South. Most likely, they too had never been so far from home.

Audiences quickly seize on commonalities and differences. The more detailed, deeply personal, and in the moment we are, the more likely we will burrow into the hearts of our listeners. Confessing mistakes, failures, and flaws endears us to audiences. They will respect our honesty, and will be more inclined to trust us.

Competent speakers do not read old, yellowed notes from the

podium. They stay up-to-date. In October and November 2001, I listened as many speakers explained that they had written their speech before 9/11. Their speeches smelled bad, like old fish.

Skilled speakers stay tuned into the tone of the room as they speak. If a cell phone rings or a baby cries, they may incorporate it into the speech in a way that doesn't embarrass anyone yet takes advantage of the moment. If a baby cries, they might say, "I'm just crazy about babies. I wish I could be the one to hold and comfort that little one. The crying reminds me that I want to say something about infants and television." Likewise, when a cell phone rings, they might comment, "That cell phone is a helpful reminder to talk about technology." This kind of spontaneity makes allies of every speaker's enemy: distractions.

One technique you can use to keep audiences engrossed is creating curiosity and suspense. I do this by simply saying, "I have something more to say about this that I will tell you later," or "I'll tell you the rest of the story in a few minutes." This kind of foreshadowing keeps listeners focused. The mind seeks the completion of ideas. Curiosity demands the whole story.

On a grim topic, such as aging or death, a carefully chosen joke can soften the pain. Again, just make sure the joke is kind and appropriate. Jokes about race, age, and gender can easily run amok and insult people. One time, I was introduced by the president of a club who warmed up the audience by telling a joke about two prostitutes. The middle-aged women who had come to hear me speak were appalled. As I sat beside this man on the dais, all eyes turned to me. I did not laugh or scowl. I kept my face a blank. I felt sympathy for his awkwardness, but he made it difficult for me to compliment him on his introduction, or to make the transition into my speech on eating disorders.

Stories, Stories, and Stories

With storytelling we enter the trance of the sacred. Telling stories reminds us of our humanity in this beautiful broken world.   —TERRY TEMPEST WILLIAMS

Once I attended a workshop given by Terry Tempest Williams. She encouraged us all to tell the person next to us our first memory of being outside in the natural world. When we re-formed a circle, she went around it asking each of us to tell one image from that memory. After this exercise, she asked for one word describing what the memory was about, and then one word about the feelings associated with the memory. Then we wrote a story based on our group work. Not only did most of us write good stories, we also connected our stories to one another's stories and together they seemed to become a community story about healing and the natural world.

With both written and spoken words, people remember stories. Savvy speakers tell and retell narratives that quiet a room and elicit laughter or tears. Stories are particularly effective in places where logical statements would inspire argument. If a story is well conceived and well told, listeners are likely to experience emotions that soften their positions and enable them to consider the speaker's point of view. When speakers elicit stories from their audiences, they become communities with transformative powers. I often ask my audiences to share stories about parenting, or the effects of television on their children, or even shopping for children. As people talk, they realize how much they share certain experiences that they felt were theirs alone.

A compelling way to begin a speech is by explaining how you learned about a topic and why you are interested in it. Most powerful ideas come from an epiphany of some sort, and that makes a good opening story. For example, Jimmy Carter tells of watching thousands of caribou migrating across Alaska. After that magical experience, he set aside more wilderness areas for Denali National Park. Or Sister Helen Prejean begins her speeches by talking about her own experiences visiting a death row inmate.

The core of a powerful speech is its logical argument, buttressed by facts, quotes, stories, poetry, and jokes. Use statistics sparingly. If something is common knowledge, do not bother documenting it. For example, there is no point offering statistics to support the point that old people are ill more often than young people, or that people live longer if they have a healthy lifestyle. We all know these things.

If the spine of a speech is strong and straight, you will hold your audience's attention. If the logic is flawed, people will quickly drop away. I actually use an outline style I learned in elementary school, with big points A, B, and C, and little numbered points beneath. That outline needs to be as logical as a theorem. You will want to find ways to highlight and summarize your key ideas. One way is repetition, although this must be skillfully done or it sounds as if you are just repeating yourself. I often say, "I will tell you my main point three times," and then I do just that. Or you can emphasize your most important points by saying, "Here is what I want you to carry home from tonight's address." Or "If you only remember two things about my talk tonight, here is what I hope they are."

It can be effective to associate your ideas with heroes. "What would Jesus do?" can be a thought-provoking question. As you suggest a course of action, if you can mention that Thomas Jefferson, Gandhi, or Václav Havel have recommended this same course you might increase your credibility. On the other hand, examples in which ordinary people are heroes may be more likely to motivate our fellow mortals than stories of Jefferson, Gandhi, or Havel. I like to quote my mother or my aunt Grace, who knew a great deal about human relationships and coping. Lately, I have been telling a story about a young woman I know named Sarah who was shopping for a sweater at a mall, and when she was about to purchase one she turned to her friends and said, "I don't really need a ninety-dollar cashmere sweater. I am going to send this money to hurricane relief instead."

To establish your humanity, quote your next-door neighbors, your grandchildren, your coworkers, or your pharmacist. A friend told me that after 9/11, her daughter Raina asked her, "What will happen if President Bush is killed by the terrorists?" My friend explained that Vice President Cheney would take over. Raina continued, "But what if he is killed too?" My friend wasn't totally up on the rules of succession, but she carefully explained that after the vice president there would be others waiting in the wings to govern our country. Then Raina asked, "What will children do if the terrorists kill all the grown-ups?" Her mother answered, "You children will need to take care of each other." That answer calmed Raina. I tell this story to show that children are quite frightened about world events, and that good parents both tell the truth and offer children ideas about how to be strong.

Quotations can make a speech shimmer, but they must be well chosen and carefully attributed. They should connect to core ideas and not be told just because they are beautiful. You do not want to use them too frequently or listeners will lose the thread of your own voice. Warnings aside, quotations give your audiences variety in voice, and they connect you with people across time and space.

Quoting writers establishes your authority as a good reader, and allows you to benefit from other people's language. In speeches about my book *Another Country,* I cite Wallace Stegner, who wrote, "We were going to leave our mark on the world and the world instead left marks on us." He expresses what we all feel, that some of our dreams died, and that life was harder than we expected it to be.

Your whole speech can be viewed as creative framing of issues of relevance to your audience. Within this frame are new questions, hypotheses, ideas, and possibilities for action. Early in your speeches, call attention to issues and problems. Later, focus on solutions. The frame itself should lead the audience members into their own fresh thinking. Thomas Friedman is quite good at this technique. The frame developed in his book *The World Is Flat* is that with globalism, nationalism, class, and distance, boundaries are fading away. Friedman's frame is provocative and generative. It is a conversation starter, even if that conversation is an argument.

Be sure to make some hopeful remarks. While despair is enervating, hope is energizing. Environmentalist Donella Meadows was asked often how much time remained to save the world. Her answer was always the same: "We have just enough time." As a change agent, you want people to believe that their actions matter. No one is powerless unless they believe themselves to be. As speakers, you have tremendous potential to engage people and set them to work. Most of your power comes from simply believing in them, and being able to honestly say to them, "You can do it."

End your speech with a call to action. Your ending should weave all your points together, and give the audience a rallying cry. On June 3, 2004, at New York University, Bill Moyers addressed the gap between rich and poor in America. He discussed inequities in education, health care, and workplaces. He ended with a great call to action: "Get mad, yes—there's plenty to be mad about. Then get organized and get busy. This is the fight of our lives."

Many speakers roar through a powerful speech but falter at the closing. Audience members leave thinking that the speaker made good points, but they don't know what to do to help. You want to help your listeners "merge deed and creed," as Thoreau referred to it. You can recommend actions that require different levels of engagement, from sending an e-mail to donating significant amounts of time and money. Be sure to suggest volunteering opportunities that cover a wide range of skills. Some people are great envelope stuffers, while others are skilled at writing press releases, creating a Web site, or contributing scientific research that supports your cause. The big message of a speech should be: We have a job for you.

The more various the solutions, the more likely that listeners will find one of them appealing. You can suggest that they chat with family and friends about whom they are voting for and why, or that they consider purchasing green products, or that they organize a march or a rally in their town to protest a policy. Be specific. Whenever possible, pass around a petition or the hat. Post sign-up sheets for work. Point out members of the audience who can answer questions about exactly what to do to help with projects. Offer people addresses, Web sites, reading lists, and the names of mentors and consultants. Make sure everyone leaving your event has a way to start working.

Close your speech with something inspirational, such as a quotation, story, or proverb. Sometimes I use the Ethiopian proverb "When spiderwebs unite, they can tie up a lion." Or I will just say something encouraging, like a good mother does when she bids her children good-bye, such as "Be kind to one another." I might say, "We underestimate each other's basic goodness. Together, we can solve these problems." Lately, I have been ending speeches by saying, "The two most radical things you can do in America are to slow down, and to talk to each other. If you do these things, you will improve our country."

Delivery

That which is spoken from the heart is heard by the heart.

—JEWISH SAYING

People cannot stand too much reality.   —CARL JUNG

I heard the daughter of a Russian leader speak in Lincoln the same week the Berlin Wall came down. She had a unique point of view about the wall, but her delivery was so lackluster that most of the audience did not stay tuned in to hear it. Recently, a Pulitzer Prize–winning writer lectured at our university. She had written a profound essay, but she read it in a monotone, never looking at the audience. Effective speakers do not "phone it in." Energy begets energy.

The time span of a speech is of paramount importance. When you have complex, multifaceted ideas, short speeches are agonizing to write. With fifty minutes, you can develop your ideas more fully and gracefully; with ten minutes, you must leave so much out. Yet we should remember the effectiveness of the short speeches Lincoln wrote for Gettysburg and his second inaugural. Short can be powerful. For most of us, speaking longer than fifty minutes takes us into dangerous territory. Research on attention span suggests we humans are all limited to about fifty minutes' concentration no matter how compelling the event. Beyond that we start yawning, or wanting a cinnamon roll, or a bathroom, or thinking about our cell phones. If I must speak longer than fifty minutes, I say, "I know you are getting restless, but I'd like to take five more minutes." I never speak more than an hour without some kind of break.

If you are a well-organized speaker, you can pack a great deal into that fifty minutes. To keep readers engaged, vary the modalities, moving from text to letters, poems, quotes, and stories. Dynamics have a great deal to do with effectiveness. Evoke a mixture of moods, moving from earnest to humorous to poignant. Contrasts hold people's attention. A good speech elicits joy, empathy, sorrow, outrage, and hope.

When speakers are anxious, they often speed through their talks. I have never heard a speaker speak too slowly. Speakers may be dull, but it's not because of the tempo of their speeches. Rather, disorganized or sketchy content, repetition, dull tone, and lack of energy lose audiences. I heard on NPR that when President Clinton was leaving office, he met with President-elect Bush, who asked him only one question, "Do you have any tips on public speaking?" Clinton answered, "Slow down. Count to three at the end of every sentence. Breathe long at every comma. You cannot go too slowly."

At the end of a speech, you want to thank your audiences for something—for caring enough to come out in the snow, for being especially good listeners, or for asking intelligent questions. When the speech is finished, stand at the podium, make eye contact, and smile at the audience for one last time. If you have done your job well, they will be applauding, and that will give you an opportunity to acknowledge your connection to them.

Stage Fright

One sleety November night, my husband and his band members were carrying their equipment into a fancy hotel ballroom for a gala event. They were slipping in the mud, getting splattered and chilled. Jim said, "This sure isn't very glamorous." The drummer responded, "Nothing is glamorous." He was absolutely right. Glamour is in the eyes of the beholder. Performers sweat, dread, worry, and just plain exhaust themselves. Audiences applaud when they make it look easy.

Public speaking is a weird mixture of stress, drudgery, and moments of grace. I have had my ups and downs. In late winter 1995, I embarked on my first book tour. I flew around the country on flights often delayed by snow and ice. I stayed alone in hotels in cities where I couldn't walk after dark. One night, trying to find the news on the television, I located one porno channel after another. As naked, gyrating bodies flashed across the screen, I cringed in almost physical pain. Then I happened onto a Lawrence Welk rerun, and relaxed with gratitude at something so cornball and midwestern. I was in rough shape that night.

I missed my family, my cats, my office, and my own bathtub. I developed sleep problems and dizziness from the stress of public speaking. Once, in the Chicago airport, waiting for a flight to Providence, I heard the last call for a flight to my hometown. I wept by its gate.

I almost bailed from the tour. But then my daughter called, and she read me Cynthia Ozick's "The Shawl," a beautiful story about a toddler who is killed by a guard in a Nazi camp just as she says her first word, "Mama." Probably, I would have cried at this story any time, but, in my crispy state, I was wrecked by it. I couldn't stop sobbing.

I cried because I was alone, anxious, and exhausted. For the first time in my life, I understood the phrase "My nerves are shot." But I also cried because that story helped me make a hard decision about continuing my tour. Nothing on earth made me feel sadder than seeing potential wasted. As a therapist, I was seeing young girls silenced before they could develop their own rich voices. That was what the *Reviving Ophelia* tour became for me. I wanted to help young girls blossom. I thank Cynthia Ozick, whom I have never met, for reminding me to keep doing my job.

Most of my life, I have been terrified of making speeches. As a girl, I lost my voice when I was forced to stand in front of a group. In high school, I was so overwrought about a required speech course that my mother wrote me a "health" excuse. During my undergraduate years, I rarely spoke in class, and I dreaded presentations. I would write a thirty-page paper to avoid a five-minute oral report.

In graduate school, I ran out of ways to run. I needed money from a teaching position, and my professors disapproved of psychology students who were too shy to teach. I was assigned a course on human sexuality. My class consisted of 175 undergraduates crowded into a hot auditorium to hear eighteen weeks of my wisdom on sexual behavior. Yikes!

The first day, I was so nervous I smoked two cigarettes at the same time. (This was in 1973, when teachers and students smoked in classrooms.) My voice trembled and faded. My knees buckled and I clung to the podium. I was red-faced and sweaty, but I made it through, and the next class was a little easier. My anxiety was exacerbated because I began the course with anatomy, which had me using words like "penis," "intercourse," and "vulva" my first week of teaching. But after I learned to discuss sex in front of a large group of giggly undergrads, I was more or less ready for anything.

By the end of the semester, I liked teaching. I knew my students, and I cared about what they learned. I no longer felt nervous in front of them; I felt pumped. I could focus on my content and my audience rather than on my own fraying nerves.

A few lucky speakers experience no stage fright, but most of us do. I am amazed by the number of famous people who have confessed that they had panic attacks or threw up before going onstage. Standing in front of dozens or hundreds of pairs of eyes, feeling pressure to hold an audience's interest, and knowing that your every word and gesture is being judged—this is an inherently alarming situation.

Two laws of the universe seem to be: Not everyone will like you or your message, and there is always one guy in the front row fast asleep with his mouth wide open. Remind yourself that people who question your ideas allow you to develop them more fully. Nevertheless, disrespectful people can be a trial. Out of every hundred people who come to hear you, at least one will be terribly difficult. Expect that.

Questions and Answers

Speakers are often jet-lagged, tired, hungry, overworked, and nervous. Then, after the speech, we are expected to work without a net by participating in questions and answers. Sometimes, we are blasted by people who carry a great deal of anger that has nothing to do with us or our topic. However, no matter what happens, we must remain accepting and nonjudgmental in our responses to questions. Every answer we give represents our attitudes toward the people in the room. If we insult a questioner, we insult the audience, and if we respect each questioner we are thought to respect the audience as a whole.

I have seen speakers alienate their audience by speaking sarcastically, by expressing contempt or defensiveness, or by belittling an audience member. Hauteur can be embedded in our content, but more often it sneaks in with style. Facial expression, body language, and tone can convey a sense of superiority. Nothing turns off an audience faster than feeling talked down to. Dropping names, telling an audience how important you are, or suggesting that you have the one right point of view are all off-putting.

Be an idealist but not a big dealist. As the old saying goes, "The world is divided into people who think they are right." Don't lose sight of the fact that there are many good causes, and you do not have a corner on truth. When my brother Jake was five, he answered what he considered a hard question, then asked my mother in all sincerity, "I know almost everything now, don't I?" Jake could be forgiven for his attitude, but speakers who harbor such illusions are generally not effective.

I try to find something to respect in all questions or comments. Even if a questioner is not very eloquent, I can usually honestly comment on their passion for the issue. When people often suggest that I write on a certain subject of interest to them, I try to empower them to take on the topic themselves.

If a question is terribly weird—for example, "What do women in the Middle East say about their vaginas?" (Yes, I really did get that question one time in Vancouver)—it's best to reframe it into something that allows a dignified response. In that case, I said, "Perhaps you are asking about education concerning reproductive health," and then I hurried on to answer my own question.

You want to give yourself permission to say, "That is outside my area of expertise," or simply, "I don't know." This is not only sensible, it actually helps establish credibility and rapport. When you are genuinely humble, you are being honest and not defensive. Audiences don't expect us to know everything. And who *does* know everything? Only know-it-alls.

It is wise to end a question-and-answer session following a positive question to which you have given a reasonably good answer. You want your audience's last view of you and your topic to be favorable.

After you speak, people will often want to share their stories. Listen closely. They are offering you a gift that you should accept graciously. And you may be able to give their gift to others you meet along the way.

Presence

Good speakers, like tall mountains, create their own weather systems. What determines the weather of a speech is presence. For speakers, presence has to do with kindness, with expression, tone of voice, carriage, tempo, level of engagement, and even with breathing. Powerful presences radiate energy.

Unlike delivery, presence is not a set of skills, and it cannot be learned in a linear way. Presence can be cultivated by self-exploration, focus, and attention. It is about the depth of your soul, your character, and your yearning to connect, and it can be summarized as the ability to be wholly present in the hearts and minds of others. Thich Nhat Hanh distinguishes between "image teaching," which uses words and ideas, and "substance teaching," which is communicated by the way you live. Presence is "substance teaching."

The world is filled with wonderful speakers, each with his or her own way of winning a crowd. Maya Angelou booms out her poetry in a voice like God's. Cornel West spellbinds groups with his brilliant, old-fashioned oratory. Jean Kilbourne's rock-solid knowledge convinces her audiences of the rightness of her causes. Carol Bly spins stories from the most common of elements—a cat, a teapot, or a flat tire—with an exquisite sense of timing and suspense.

The largest component of presence may be tone of voice. In America today, the shrill, the bombastic, the hysterical, and the sensational often are the voices that are heard. While I write this, I think with dismay about mean-spirited talk radio shock jocks. They seem to be effective at gaining an audience, but they don't make our world a better place. Their derision and ridicule degrade the culture for us all. This kind of speech is the opposite of what I advocate. Hate speech objectifies, dehumanizes, and leads to bad behavior, including hurting the dehumanized without guilt. It is antithetical to I-thou speech, which leads to civil discourse, and is the social cement necessary to preserve this house called America.

Eleanor Roosevelt, much vilified by political enemies in her day, always spoke respectfully of others. Her guidelines for public life are relevant to speech making: "Develop skin as tough as a rhino's hide. You cannot take anything personally. You cannot bear grudges. You must finish the day's work when the day's work is done. Don't be easily discouraged. Take defeat over and over, pick yourself up and go on."

Raymond Carver once wrote of a character, "She liked people and they liked her back." All of us are more likely to be influenced by speakers we find sympathetic. However, being likable is complicated. It doesn't mean hiding all our flaws. Defensive or perfect people are not all that appealing. Authenticity is key. My best advice is to love your audiences. Be present with them. Form a small community in the time you have together. If you love them as neighbors and family members, they will know it, and they will allow you into their hearts. Then you can create moments for them in which transformation is possible.

THIRTEEN

PERSONAL ESSAYS

> Change occurs when deeply felt private experiences are given public legitimacy. —GANDHI
>
> Ten times a day something happens to me like this—some strengthening throb of amazement—some good sweet empathic ping and swell. This is the first, the wildest and the wisest thing I know: that the soul exists and is built entirely out of attentiveness. —MARY OLIVER
>
> Viewed from the distance of the moon, the astonishing thing about the earth, catching the breath, is that it's alive.
>
> —LEWIS THOMAS

Every time I shop for groceries, I am confronted by a host of health, environmental, and human rights issues. I want to avoid sugar, trans fats, and sodium, but the labeling is deliberately confusing. I don't buy blueberries from Chile in February, but I can't figure out where the celery comes from. I struggle to discern which bananas were picked by well-paid workers, which were not sprayed with deadly insecticides. I want to buy milk without hormones, and fish whose populations are not depleted or factory-farmed in a polluting way. I want to drink shade-grown, fair-trade coffee, but as I scrutinize labels I don't know whom to trust. No one is really monitoring the situation. We need an international certification and regulation program for all food production. Can a personal essay lug that big idea in the container of my trip to the grocery store?

Thich Nhat Hanh writes about relative truth and absolute truth. Relative truth is the wave; absolute truth is the ocean. When we write a good personal essay, we become aware that our wave of truth is part of the bigger ocean of truth.

Personal essays connect the events in our personal lives to greater world events. A man serving soup at a homeless shelter, a teenager watching reality television with her friends, a middle-aged couple visiting a neighbor in the hospital—any of these events could inspire a profound personal essay. In such essays, we describe a precise moment in time in a way that includes everything we know about the world. The deeper we dive into our own experience, and the more honest and insightful we are in reporting, the more we connect to all other humans.

Juxtapositions often lead us to profound personal essays. For example, a friend told me she was at the airport watching a CNN broadcast of New Orleans's flooding while, right in front of the television screen, a group of teenage girls on their way to a cheerleading contest were laughing and practicing their cheers. Recently, I was giving a speech at a small college while a close friend was undergoing open-heart surgery. As I thought about my friend on the operating table, I listened to a band play warm-up polka music with goat-skinned bagpipes, a drum, and a sousaphone. Either of these juxtapositions, fully explored, could inspire personal essays.

In Adam Gopnick's essay "Waiting for Mr. Ravioli," he observes his daughter relating to her imaginary friend. He is astounded to realize that she never actually imagines that her friend is in the room with her. She pages Mr. Ravioli, leaves a message on his answering machine, and, rarely, speaks with him on the phone to say that she is just too busy to see him. Gopnick uses this poignant story to discuss Americans' "busyness," and their lack of leisure time for family and friends. His essay is touchingly funny, yet it captures a deep truth about all of our lives circa 2006.

After listening to the Minneapolis Symphony perform Brahms's Tragic Overture and Alban Berg's Violin Concerto, Bill Holm wrote a personal essay, "Long-Hair Music for an America at War." In it, he reflects on the difference between the tragic worldview embedded in all great works of music or literature and Americans' can-do optimism. "Americans prefer to keep tragedy and grief far away from public consciousness," Holm writes.

He concludes with a story about visiting a friend, Icelandic pianist Jonas Ingimundarsson, who was a cancer survivor. Ingimundarsson told him, "Now I have time only for the most beautiful music." Ingimundarsson played a Chopin nocturne, then one of Schubert's last *Klavierstucke*. Holm wrote, "I wept like an idiot listening to him." He ends his essay this way: "None of us has time for any but the most beautiful music, the greatest music, played and heard with everything inside us. Nor does the United States."

Listening to music, Bill Holm was able to connect his own emotions to our nation's emotional need to open ourselves up to our pain and sorrow, to weep, and then return to the world whole and ready to help. Only by facing our own grief fully can we do the work necessary to alleviate the world's grief. And Holm, being a fine poet, expresses all these sentiments in beautiful language.

With personal essays, we turn our own lives into teachable moments for others. Sometimes, we simplify the story for our readers. We sort through a raft of information on government-subsidized food programs for schools and boil it all down to a simple question: Will Johnny and Lucy from across the highway get fed healthy meals at school? Or we study global warming and climate change, and ask: Does this mean my white pines will die?

Other times, we let small events embody the complexities of large issues. A pop bottle washed up on the beach can lead to a discussion of pollution in the ocean and the death of coral reefs and fish species. A child without a warm coat, walking down a snowy street, inspires us to write about poverty. Driving by a school between an adult bookstore and a liquor store spurs an essay on zoning laws.

With personal essays, we invite the world to join us in our epiphany. We share real details and experiences, yet we weave our very souls into our stories. We enable a finite moment to transcend itself, opening up our readers and ourselves to a whole new understanding of the universe.

Feeling Out of Control?
Lynda Madison, Ph.D.

My husband and I tiled our kitchen this weekend. I liked it (and, surprisingly, it looks okay too). But while I was running the saw, splitting the tiles, and slapping on glue, it occurred to me that a project like that can be pretty darned therapeutic for a parent. I mean, raising children is a job that takes years to show results. You can feel like you have no control (which isn't true, by the way). And it's tough to know at any given moment if you're doing it right: Are the kids too active? Too quiet? Too involved? Not engaged? Too concerned? Not worried enough? Likewise, a parent's primary feedback comes from the children themselves, which, let's face it, can be a little unrewarding at times. What occurred to me this weekend is that doing something creative—like writing or painting or tiling a kitchen—lets you lose yourself in the creative process. It puts you "in the zone" for a little while, where you don't think about all your daily concerns, and, somehow, you come out refreshed. Having a creative project can even show the kids that there's more to life than television. I don't know why I liked *tiling* so much, though. I think it's because I got messy on purpose, made a whole lot of noise and shaped those little pieces *my* way. I put them right where I wanted them and, by gosh, they stayed there. Just the kind of control every parent needs now and then. Now, don't all rush to the hardware store at once . . .

Madison's essay is witty and yet poignant. As she shares a small story about tiling her kitchen, she connects to the almost universal issue of parental loss of control over their children's lives.

In her personal essay "A Hundred Seeds," Kelly Madigan Erlandson writes about how if feels to be an alcoholic in recovery, working in a treatment program. She wrote it after a drunk driver injured her cousin.

When a nurse who had never met my cousin laid down next to her in the dirt road, she offered us a way to begin to make sense of the loss. She stood in for us, and I don't know if I would have done the same. I have no doubt, however, that I could have been the one behind the wheel, either in Mexico or on that dark Nebraska highway on Thanksgiving Day. If so, I don't imagine I'd have wanted to be bailed or bribed out of jail. No life jacket of kapok or milkweed could have pulled me to safety again. The weight of my actions would surely drag me to the bottom.

Every year in January, the Alumni Association of the treatment center where I work throws a Chili Feed and invites everyone who has ever been through treatment with us. Between four hundred and five hundred people usually show up. There are various awards presented and speeches made, and recognition of the people sitting in that rented hall who have transformed, and are transforming, their lives. It's a noisy crowd, but before all the formal talk gets going, we observe a moment of silence for those we refer to as "the still suffering."

The silence washes the edges of the room. I think of myself so many years ago. I think of the men who have come through treatment but couldn't find their way into sobriety. I think of the Driver, somewhere in Mexico, and I say a prayer for him, and for his parents.

There is this. When my cousin was in her Golden Hour, a stranger came to be with her. She lay down in the hot street beside her, and she didn't leave. When Julie couldn't breathe, she blew breath across her face to calm her.

And there is this. From where I am now, I see the young girl that I was, out of her senses, one eye closed, billowing down the road toward the river in a 1973 Buick, so utterly and hopelessly unaware. I climb in next to her. I tell her help is coming. I don't know if she can hear me. I tell her again.

In this candid essay, Madigan Erlandson skillfully connects her own experiences as a recovering alcoholic, as a counselor, and as a family member of someone injured by a drunk driver. As she weaves these points of view together, she opens our eyes and hearts to the pain of all involved. The essay is about a specific event and ideas related to alcoholism, yet in the end it touches on the most profound issues: healing, personal responsibility, and forgiveness. Her ending weaves all the strands of the story together.

Suzuki music teacher Pam Barger writes to inspire her students to practice. Here is a small section from one of her many essays as a music teacher.

On Practicing Piano
PIANO PRACTICE AS A PROBLEM-SOLVING ADVENTURE
Pam Herbert Barger

Let me begin with two stories.

The first one's on me. I confess that when I was a kid, I hated to practice. I loved to *play* piano—pieces that I already knew and loved. But just thinking about practice gave me, more than anything, a feeling of dread. Looking back, I think the dread came from picturing myself plowing through something I was no good at. Who wants to struggle?

This other story is one I read years ago in a Suzuki magazine. The writer of the article was interviewing children who had made quick progress through the Suzuki books. She asked a twelve-year-old in Japan who already had finished *all* the books how much time he spent practicing every day. "About ten minutes," was the answer the stunned writer heard.

The young man went on to say that after he practiced, he *played* the piano for an hour or more.

It wasn't until I was about fifteen that I learned to practice well. I loved a certain Bach invention, but I just plain couldn't get through it without proper fingering. Finally it occurred to me that if I actually *worked* at getting the fingering right, bit by bit, I might be able to play the piece. Of all things, it didn't take especially long to do it right, and it was great fun to play that piece fast and without those annoying mistakes.

Right around that time, I tried out for the select choir at my high school and didn't make it! I guess I just assumed I could count on that one. I was crushed, but decided to make the best of it. Mom found me a voice teacher, and I set about doing exactly what the teacher said, every darned day, for at least forty minutes.

I was amazed at how quickly I could hear results. When I tried out again that December, I was in. Within a year I found myself singing professionally, something that I still manage to do some thirty-two years later.

Barger is practical, insightful, and humble. She strikes just the right tone for addressing her students: respectful, witty, and relaxed. As Barger recommends fresh ways to think about practicing, she suggests small, manageable steps, and she ends her piece with an excellent call to action: "Amaze me. Amaze your parents. Amaze yourself!"

> Find your place on the planet, dig in and take responsibility from there.
> —GARY SNYDER

Personal essays allow us to struggle on paper with our deepest questions, and then to share that struggle with others. Because they allow us to reflect on the meaning of our experiences, many of us find them profoundly satisfying to write. You may want to experiment with this form by finding something every day that inspires you to write a personal essay. If you do, you will find that the quality of your attention will improve.

The first step in all writing is observation. You notice something, say, the long lines of old people waiting for flu shots at the drugstore. Then you record what you observed. Note the old gentleman with his shiny brown suit, his belt cinching the pants just a few inches below his bow tie. Describe the woman in a frayed blue sweater leaning on her walker. Depict the red-faced man moving his oxygen tank along with him in the line for the nurse. Note the store manager finding a few chairs for the group to share. Write about the kindness with which these chairs are allocated. Record the tired faces, the support hose, the swollen ankles, the broken blood vessels on noses. Note the little boy who stares, the clerk who brings the old man water, the old man's sighs, and the people who leave the line because they can't stand up any longer.

Later, at your desk, keep writing. Ask yourself, Why did I find this scene so moving? Why do I want to share this story with others? What am I trying to achieve? Describe your observations and experiences, or view your experience as a metaphor for something greater. Once you have a sense for a deeper meaning, elaborate.

Sometimes, the meaning of a moment is clear as we experience it. Other times, it is hard-won, discovered only after laborious efforts to make sense of our experience. But in a good essay, the epiphany will come. Personal essays follow a simple pattern: We share our epiphany with others, and, voilà, the world is changed.

FOURTEEN

BLOGS—A REVOLUTIONARY
NEW TOOL

Intelligent people can always come up with intelligent reasons to do nothing. —SCOTT SIMON

We are confronted with insurmountable opportunities.
—POGO

B logs surfaced in the 1990s as online journals for people who worked with computer technology, but they quickly morphed into a much bigger phenomenon. Computer users began posting personal blogs that included everything from daily activities to poetry, travel tips, movie reviews, political commentary, and thoughts about the universe.

On 9/11, political blogs were just emerging, but, after 9/11, the numbers of bloggers exploded. All over the world, people wanted to share their thoughts and feelings. By 2005, sixteen percent of our citizens, or thirty-two million people, read blogs daily, and one out of seventeen Americans maintains a blog. (All these statistics are taken from *The Pew/Internet Report Buzz*, "Blogs and Beyond," May 16, 2005.)

My friend Steve, who writes a blog about legal issues for attorneys, is rather typical. On his blog, he shares op-ed pieces, book and movie reviews, recipes, and excerpts from other blogs. Steve reads about fifty blogs a day, and he estimates that a hundred people read his blog daily. He follows several blogs out of Baghdad, his favorite being by a young woman who lives in the center of the city, riverbendblog.blogspot.com. She posts only intermittently because of problems with electricity, but she is an amazing chronicler of events from an Iraqi point of view. Her blog has been published by the Feminist Press of the City University of New York. Another blog, dear_raed.blogspot.com, comes from a young man who was eventually hired by the *London Guardian* to cover the war. Still another, secretsinbaghdad.blogspot.com, is by a student at Mustansiriya University who offers a poignant mix of reports on parties, movies, bombings, and the deaths of people he knows. Because of blogging, Steve has a pretty good sense of what the war in Iraq is like for ordinary people.

Writing a blog is instant self-publication, which is its own special kind of creativity. Live journals with interactive potential inspire a great deal of incisive, quirky, and voice-filled writing. Blogs seem to emphasize self-reflection and social commentary. When bloggers sit down to write, they often seem to think more deeply than usual about their place in the bigger world. And, later, they have the satisfaction of readers' reactions.

Blogs are the most democratic and widely utilized form of self-publishing. If people have access to a computer and the Internet, they can promulgate their ideas. They don't need credentials or money. There are no gatekeepers on the Internet and few access issues, at least in America, where all public libraries now have the technology available. As a vehicle of communication, blogging is immediate, open to all people, and amenable to any content. Blogs allow citizens to converse anywhere, anytime, about anything. Conversations can be political, academic, spiritual, or just plain practical. Users can both gather and disseminate ideas. Blogs allow communities of kindred spirits— dog lovers, vegetarians, pediatricians, quilters, and writers to be in touch. With eight hundred million people worldwide with Internet access, blogging will continue to spread and flourish.

Like any other medium, blogs are not without their drawbacks. There are vile hate- and fear-spewing blogs. Terrorist groups, criminals, and racists can connect over the Web and work more efficiently. Recipes for bomb building, political enemies' lists, information on buying illegal weapons, and child pornography can be found on the Web. There is no quality control. Ill-considered reactions, misinformation, financial chicanery, and sleazy sexuality are almost impossible to avoid. Over time, readers learn to find what they want, but the volume of information is so enormous that the retrieval and sorting of information is time-consuming. While newspapers, public radio, press releases all can be held accountable, there is no accountability on the Web. It is a frontier town, with all the disorder and lawlessness that term implies.

Still, blogs offer some things that more established media don't. Howard Rheingold's *Smart Mobs* describes the powerful forces for change that linked-together bloggers can become. These "blogo-spheres" can serve as watchdogs on media, challenging stories, and suggesting stories that are being missed. Especially "A-list" blogs— the most credible and the most widely read blogs—are a new force in American politics. This is heartening, because not just the rich and powerful but anyone eloquent and passionate can have influence. We can all be pamphleteers—modern-day Tom Paines.

Blogs can alter perceptions, change behavior, embarrass or embolden people, and affect donations and campaign coffers. The

Downing Street Minutes, which were notes about the early planning for the Iraq war, had blogs buzzing a month before the mainstream press picked up on the story.

Newsweek publishes a weekly *Blogwatch. The Drudge Report* and the gossipy, politically in the know blog *Wonkette* are read by Capitol Hill insiders every morning right along with *The Washington Post.*

Bloggers report on the stories that major news media do not cover—not because these stories are insignificant, but because they are too politically loaded. They comment on events, criticize leaders and policies, organize protests and campaigns, raise money, and inform others of gatherings and opportunities to change the world. Many people read blogs so they can come to understand issues from multiple points of view, and they themselves blog to discuss their points of view with people all over the world.

When I read blogs from hot spots around the world, I am struck by how close I feel. After Hurricane Katrina, for example, my favorite news source was a professor at Xavier University in New Orleans who kept a daily journal online about what he and his friends were going through. He is still writing about the aftereffects— the odors, the mold and rot, and the insurance problems—at michaelhoman.blogspot.com.

Many American soldiers are writing home from Iraq with very different accounts than those we see on the front pages of our newspapers. In *The Washington Post,* Jonathan Finer shared the following entry.

There were no reporters riding shotgun on the highway north of Baghdad when a roadside bomb sent Sgt. Elizabeth Le Bel's Humvee lurching into a concrete barrier. The Army released a three-sentence statement about the incident in which her driver, a fellow soldier, was killed. Most news stories that day noted it briefly. But a vivid account of the attack appeared on the Internet within hours of the Dec. 4 crash. Unable to sleep after arriving at the hospital, Le Bel hobbled to a computer and typed 1,000 words of what she called "my little war story" into her Web log, or blog, titled "Life in this Girl's Army," at http://www.sgtlizzie.blogspot.com/. "I started to scream bloody murder, and one of the other females on the convoy came over, grabbed my hand and started to calm me down. She held onto me, allowing me to place my leg on her shoulder as it was hanging free," Le Bel wrote. "I thought that my face had been blown off, so I made the remark that I wouldn't be pretty again LOL. Of course the medics all rushed with reassurance which was quite amusing as I know what I look like now and I don't even want to think about what I looked like then." Her Web site has received about 45,000 hits since she started it a year ago.

Finer reported that blogs like this are becoming so influential that they are subject to military censorship.

Blogs may become this new century's major form of social protest. Citizens will let their fingers do the walking. While there is a different kind of power in protest marches—in being with all kinds of people, in singing and listening to speeches, and in sharing meals and blankets—blogs have many equivalent functions: gathering signatures for petitions, demonstrating the strength of a movement, keeping the faithful posted, inspiring actions, and empowering the powerless.

Social activists of all stripes have discovered the power of blogs as electronic calls to action; thousands of supporters can be rallied quickly. Blogs are particularly good for urgent-action alerts. When a bill is on the Senate floor, when a rally protesting it has been planned for Saturday morning, or when budget cuts to social programs happen overnight, blogs spread the word to interested parties in nanoseconds.

After the Asian tsunami, I received dozens of suggestions about where I could send money. One, "I'm Okay But Sri Lanka Is Not," from Vicki Robin, coauthor of *Your Money or Your Life,* posed the question, "How much do I think you should send? Look at the pictures again. Put yourself in the place of someone who just lost everything. What would you want from someone like you? After my own personal disaster regarding my health, I can't afford to send anything. However, I will be sending a check for 1,000 dollars. How much should you send? Send more than you think you can afford." After reading her appeal, I doubled my donation.

Howard Dean's presidential campaign was blog driven. MoveOn.org organized citizens to work in concert for common cause. It was launched during the Clinton impeachment hearings by two Silicon Valley entrepreneurs with no political experience. They were frustrated by the partisan warfare in D.C., and they wanted to build a network of citizens to discuss important issues. Within days, hundreds of people signed up. MoveOn.org PAC's executive director is twenty-four years old, but people of all ages visit the site and engage in lively discussions. This blog's most important contribution may well be that it has increased many citizens' level of engagement in the political process.

Blogs are conversation cafés and technological speakers' corners. They offer people of the world voices in a great dialogue that could help build communities, sometimes international ones, of people who do similar kinds of work. They are tangible manifestations of the central fact of the universe: Everything is connected.

Blogs offer us zero degrees of separation from people anywhere and everywhere. We can "hear" the voices of ordinary citizens reporting their stories. With blogs, we can build I-thou relationships with people very different from ourselves. Over time, blogs will continue to connect us, teach us empathy, and perhaps even save us from ourselves.

FIFTEEN

MUSIC AND POETRY

Step by step,
the longest march,
can be won,
can be won.　　　　—OLD UNION SONG

This we know:
All things are connected
Like the blood
Which unites one family.
Whatever befalls the earth
Befalls the sons and daughters of the earth.
Man did not weave the web of life:
He is merely a strand in it.
Whatever he does to the web,
He does to himself.　　—CHIEF SEATTLE

M usic and poetry are transformative tools that connect us to each other and to ourselves. Since the dawn of human history, we have created song and verse. The Chinese and Japanese have composed poetry for thousands of years, as have the Greeks, the Persians, and the Icelandic people. Indeed, poetry offers us a history of human emotions. For over two millennia, people have memorized the Psalms, some of the finest poetry and music ever composed. Even today, living as we do far from our animal rhythms, our tribes, and our ancient traditions, music and poetry can carry us back home.

This is not a chapter on how to write a song or poem. Rather, it is a sampling of work that has moved me. And while good songs and poems can stand alone on their literary merits, both also can connect us to broader cultural issues.

Music

> Music makes practically everybody fonder of life than he or she would be without it.   —KURT VONNEGUT

Music plays a major role in all cultures. Historically, music has brought us together, roused us to action, inspired us to persevere, soothed us, or presented us with visions of a better world. Some anthropologists believe that music may predate speech. As a species, we have composed songs for work, community building, prayer, love, birth, and death.

The auditory circuits that carry music to the brain are proximate to that part of the brain that controls emotions. Music causes both to vibrate, and literally moves us to feelings. Because music burrows so deeply into our psyches, singing adds power and richness to words. Test this theory for yourself by reciting, then singing, "Glory! Glory, Hallelujah."

Music is connected to memory in different ways than is speech. Alzheimer's patients who no longer remember their names can still sing songs. People in deep comas often can respond to music. Songs transport us back to our mother's cradling, our first day at school, making out in our parents' basements, or our trip to the ocean. Songs carry us back in time to the Civil War, the Irish potato famine, the early days on the Great Plains, the Great Depression, or World War II. The lullabies we sing to our children come from our grandmothers, who more than likely learned them from their grandmothers.

Music taps into the galaxies within us all. And music entrains our rhythms with those of other people, causing us to breathe together. Singing together builds community instantly. Singing in harmony literally creates harmony. Pete Seeger said, "Singing together you find out that there are things you can learn from each other that you can't learn from arguments or any other way."

After the nuclear accident at Chernobyl, the elm trees there died from nuclear fallout. As the people forced out of the area gathered on the peripheries of their homeland, they sang and danced "The Elm Dance." After September 11, I sang this same song and danced with others on a beach south of San Francisco. It has a haunting melody, and its lyrics describe trees trembling in the wind, and especially a golden apple tree that blooms in the morning mist. All over the world, people have come to appreciate these simple images from nature. "The Elm Dance" is soothing, even redemptive.

Music can melt the iced-over places in our hearts and bring forth tears and resolution. When friends die and I am numb to my own sorrow, I put on Lucinda Williams, Johnny Cash, Emmylou Harris, Solomon Burke, and Ralph Stanley. Only then can I begin to cry.

In Burundi, Rwanda, and the refugee camps of Kenya and Ghana, psychologists use music to work with the thousands of traumatized children, many without parents. Teaching children healing songs becomes a kind of group therapy for these victims of post-traumatic stress. Because music penetrates deeper than words, even deeper than pain, it is curative even in the direst of situations.

People in all times and places have appreciated the healing powers of song. Lennon and McCartney's "Let It Be" is filled with sorrow, but also a kind of solace that encourages us to accept what cannot be changed. We all have our regrets, and our need to let go of certain thoughts, feelings, and experiences. This song taps into that universal experience. As we listen, we easily can apply the words to our own lives.

Almost every important social movement has its songs. Sam Cooke sang "A Change Is Gonna Come" during the civil rights movement. "Smells Like Teen Spirit" by Nirvana was a call to consciousness and a howl of rage against corporations that buy and sell teen culture. "Big Yellow Taxi" by Joni Mitchell and "You Could Have Walked Around the World" by Butch Hancock are anthems of environmental consciousness.

As musicologist Oscar Brand put it, "Protest songs move the body, move the mind, and move the government." He considered "We Shall Overcome" a perfect protest song. It is easy to sing, and it evokes strong emotions. And it is so general that it can be sung for almost every cause. I would also nominate the Carter Family's version of "Will the Circle Be Unbroken" as "perfect."

Think of the music of the antiwar movement of the 1960s and

'70s: "Where Have All the Flowers Gone," "I Ain't Gonna Study War No More," "Last Lonely Eagle," "Masters of War," and "Give Peace a Chance." You may not remember the words of many speeches from that era, but I'll bet you remember some of the songs.

We have our great national songwriters such as John Prine, Ani DiFranco, Bruce Springsteen, Steve Earle, and Tracy Chapman. In every town in America, music flourishes. People ages ten to a hundred write songs—about politics, injustice, poverty, war, and the environment.

If you are at all musically inclined, I encourage you to experiment with songwriting. Good songs, like good personal essays, manage to express universal ideas in plain, precise language. Melodies are easy to borrow from other songs, if you have trouble coming up with your own. Woody Guthrie called this borrowing the "folk music process."

In a rather infamous example, John Newton, captain of a slave ship, most likely borrowed the melody for "Amazing Grace" from Africans he was shipping to America. A self-proclaimed wretch, once lost now found, he experienced what he later called his "great deliverance" during a violent storm at sea. In 1748, after Newton became a minister, he wrote his hymn, and it still resonates with people all over the world today.

A good place to begin your work is with an image. For instance, "Old Rugged Cross," "Swing Low, Sweet Chariot," or Elizabeth Cotton's "Freight Train" are all built around strong images. Place-names also make very effective images. John Prine's "Paradise," about Muhlenberg County, Otis Redding's "Dock of the Bay," and Randy Newman's "Louisiana 1927" are all anchored in geographic location. Recall a story that made you weep, then try to write it out in verse. Dylan's "The Lonesome Death of Hattie Carroll," Leonard

Cohen's "Suzanne," and Townes Van Zandt's "Snowing on Raton" are all haunting story songs. Bruce Springsteen's *Nebraska,* a collection of songs based on the life of mass murderer Charles Stark-weather, is a whole album of such songs.

Songs often are inspired by intense feelings. Billie Holiday wrote "Strange Fruit" as a howl of pain about lynchings in the South, the "fruits" being the bodies of black people hanging from the trees. Other examples are Hank Williams's "I'm So Lonesome I Could Cry" and Carter Stanley's "White Dove."

When you are sad, angry, or discouraged about the world, sit down with a pen, a guitar or piano and see what happens. Of course, when you are joyous, write then too. Think of "Chelsea Morning" by Joni Mitchell, or Van Morrison's "Moondance." Begin with a metaphor that captures the exact mood you are in. Play around. Songwriters tell me that some songs fall onto their heads like rain, while others need to be tinkered with for years until they are just right.

Sometimes, songs are written to be inspiring. Dylan recorded "The Times They Are A-Changin'" two months after the death of John Kennedy. He wanted to broadcast a warning to Americans that if they didn't change they would be left behind in the dust of young people moving toward a new world order.

The best protest songs, as well as songs of celebration, are grounded in imagery. Songwriting and music making will never die because they are a means for expressing our emotions about the world. They bring us together, and they help us go on.

Poetry

A good poem can set its listener adrift in a small raft under a vast night sky of stars.   —JANE HIRSHFIELD

The poet's goal is to light up the sky.   —TED KOOSER

The poet's job is to tell the truth and nothing but the truth, in such a way that people cannot live without it; to put into words those feelings we all have that are so deep, so important, and yet so difficult to name.   —JANE KENYON

Poetry has the gossamer quality of a snowflake and the power of a sword. Writing poetry is like painting a landscape on a grain of sand. Poets write precisely and close to the bone. "Ultimately, a poem has an electrical force field which is love," says Joy Harjo.

Long after the kings and warlords are buried, and their buildings and shrines crumble and decay, and the memory of their wars fade away, we will have poetry. It is every civilization's record of itself. Omar Khayyám's *Rubaiyat,* Homer's *Odyssey,* and Shakespeare's sonnets: that's what we remember in the end.

Poetry can express collective outrage and scorn. It can bring down governments, or at least keep hope alive until they fall. At great risk, Boris Pasternak wrote samizdat, or underground poetry, to help his fellow Russians stay afloat emotionally until the Soviet Union collapsed. He and his fellow poets secretly printed poetry and passed it from hand to hand until it was nothing but tatters. Or they memorized poems and recited them in smoky cafés or working at the factory. Poetry in the USSR was the way people signaled that their souls were their own, that they, and not the government, would define their lives. Much of the rebellion against the Soviets was fueled by samizdat poetry. Poets were imprisoned and shot because of the words they wrote, and average citizens risked their own lives to read that poetry or hear it recited.

More recently, in America, wars, human rights, social and economic justice, and environmental issues have inspired poets. Poems are medicine for our troubled culture. Barbara Schmitz's short piece sums up many of her own feelings after 9/11: the wish to run away, the wish to be deeply connected to others, and the wish to learn something from the experience. Her poem made me feel less alone.

September 17, 2001

What have I learned?
When someone announces there's
been a disaster and you can
leave or stay, "Run, run, run
for your life."

What have I learned?
In times of terror,
Times of hate,
Human hearts pour forth love
From their crucibles of pain
Hands reach out to hold,
to give.

What have I learned?
To live well.
To live deep.
Drink beauty, eat life.
Look, look, look, and see.

What have I learned?
To do what I do . . .
With perfection
With joy.
Be kind.

When I interviewed older people for *Another Country,* I was often struck by how much poetry they could recite from memory. My parents' generation memorized poetry in school. Farmers, cooks, housewives, and lawyers could quote Longfellow, Wordsworth, Robert Service, or Dylan Thomas. My grandparents considered poetry one of life's important coping tools. It also was seen as a way to entertain one another, and to introduce beauty into what were essentially harsh midwestern lives. Although most people no longer memorize poetry to recite to one another at parties or on winter nights, there still are poetry readings, "slams," and workshops all over America. After all, rap is poetry. And cowboy poetry thrives in this part of the world. Creative writing programs, in fact, are filled with would-be poets. The flame burns on.

During the time I wrote *The Middle of Everywhere,* I helped a family of six Kurdish sisters and their mother. They had endured years of poverty, isolation, and now exile. As women in a Taliban-controlled country, they had been sequestered far from school, work, and entertainment. After coming to America, they spent their first months just trying to survive, finding transportation, English-language classes, health care, and jobs. But almost as soon as they got the necessities squared away, the youngest sister asked me, "Could you buy us a book of poetry?"

In the 1970s, I attended John Neihardt's last reading at the University of Nebraska Student Union. Neihardt by then was an old man. Blind, crippled, skinny in his shiny black suit, he was less than five feet tall and had flowing white hair. His daughter led him onto the stage in front of hundreds of people, and he looked so fragile that it seemed almost cruel to expect him to speak. But he just sat down, adjusted the microphone, and began to recite. Speaking slowly at first, within a few minutes he was growling like thunder.

He told of meeting his wife. She had read his poems in Paris, and his work had had such an intoxicating effect on her that she wrote him a letter, then came all the way from France to marry him sight unseen. They stayed together until her death. Of her, Neihardt said, "She wove her ways into the landscape of my life." He then recited from his book *Black Elk Speaks*. He ended with his long poem "The Death of Crazy Horse." As he recited, tears rolled down his leathery old cheeks, and also down the cheeks of most of us in the audience.

Perhaps John Neihardt was crying over the murder of Crazy Horse and the lost world of the magnificent Plains Indians. We in that crowded auditorium were crying for those reasons as well. But we also wept in awe of Neihardt's presence, and over our own anticipated loss. We knew the world would never see the likes of him again.

Poetry can be a stone, a prayer, a kiss, or a gun. Poets write to create beauty, tell the truth, speak for those without voices, comfort the sorrowful, encourage the hopeless, call attention to that which is fragile, and encourage us to be mindful. We need poets in these dark times much the same way the Russians needed theirs. You have the power to make a difference.

"Assateague Island," by Marjorie Saiser, is a poem that straddles the intersection where the personal and the political collide. She begins with an image, weaves it through her history with her son, and finally weaves their story into her sorrow over the war in Vietnam. To me, the message here is that if we can heal ourselves, we can heal the country. It's a poem about forgiveness and redemption, yet, because it subtly points the reader toward the damage done to our nation because of the war it is an activist poem as well.

Assateague Island, October

For an hour my son stands in the bluegreen ocean,
his shoes slung over his shoulder, looking east past
   the place where
in the shell-green water,
the water swells,
past the place where
the wave, though it has no beginning, begins.

Every seventh wave
against his ankles, calves, knees,
splashing up onto his old hiking shorts.
He has said the crash of the water is a breathing.

I sit on the sand. I too hear
the planet breathing
blow after blow,

my breath slows
matching.

That time when I pulled
your hair in anger. I am sorry.
Let this wave heal it. That time when
I made you, a little boy,
so carefully apologize
for what didn't matter.
Let this wave heal it.
When I didn't write you, afraid
your father would misread.
Let it be carried up
Like a handful of small white bubbles.

When I fussed over you.
When I couldn't stop
Even though you hated fussing.
Let this wave wash that.
When I talked too much
in front of your friends.
Let this water and foam
take it.
When you were in the hospital, fighting
the bars, the rails, my arms
To climb out of bed.
Let this wave take that away.

When I was busy growing up
and you needed me. Let this whole

sky-green ocean swell up
and breathe it away.

Tomorrow we will go to the
Vietnam Memorial, you and I.
It will be raining. We will stand
with others in the rain
and I will cry for the pink rose on the ground
and the old man holding a
black and white umbrella.
I will cry and you,
who do not cry,
will put your palm
like a rose
on the shoulder of my damp coat.

Name after name
name after name
rolls in us and upon us
healing you, healing me.

CODA

SEEKING STILLNESS/
INSPIRING ACTION

> The real truth is this: The whole world is joy. Heaven is a
> festival all year long. Of all lies, the greatest falsehood is
> melancholy. ——ISAAC BASHEVIS SINGER
>
> We shall awaken from our dullness and rise vigorously
> toward justice. ——HILDEGARD OF BINGEN

October 30, 2003. It is a dark morning, with sleet predicted. After a week of stomach flu, I am coming down with a cold. Jim is hacking and sniffling, and we have been a dull and cranky couple. Yesterday, we replaced the motor on our furnace, and paid an enormous health insurance premium. Our daughter called from D.C. to report that thieves had broken into her car and stolen her CD player. One close friend was diagnosed with breast cancer, another called to tell me that her son was going into alcohol treatment.

This morning, however, I sit at my desk with a cup of tea and a vase of pink roses. I begin by journaling, then I answer a business letter. Then finally, I turn to this book. I have pen, paper, and a few ideas. I lose myself in a process of thinking on paper. My little ego, which worries about bank statements and weekend plans, fades away. For a while, I vanish into a temple of words.

There is a sense in which our most intimate lifelong relationship is with our own comfort zone. When I am writing, I fall into what psychologist Mihaly Csikszentmihalyi called "flow," where I lose track of time and place, and inhabit the focused moment.

Flow can also describe a certain relationship with life—a sense of the self-evident goodness of being alive. Writing catapults me into that relationship. There is great joy in putting one's brain to work in the ordered universe of language. In a chaotic and disordered world, writing offers calmness and clarity. It opens my life to a certain capaciousness.

In *My Ántonia,* Willa Cather wrote, "This is happiness, to be dissolved into something complete and great." She was referring to the prairie sky, but she could have been referring to writing. To lose oneself in discovering, analyzing, improving, going deeper and pushing harder; that is my favorite way of dissolving.

As a girl, I was the fixer in my frenetic, disorganized household. I did the dishes, hung up the coats, and tossed out the cigarette butts and old newspapers. Whenever I could, I retreated to the public library, with its oak tables and leather books, or to school, with its waxy floors, rows of desks, and sharpened pencils.

As an adult, I am the fixer in my own family as well. The children and grandchildren arrive for Thanksgiving. We take joy in our reunion, but we share a small space physically and a complicated family history emotionally. After a while, old tensions surface, and fault lines reveal themselves. Trying to make things work in a universe I cannot control, I grow anxious. We have fun, but it's messy family fun, filled with shared stories and disagreements, with laughter and hurt feelings, emotional crashes and hugs.

I will look forward to the time when I can return to my sanctuary, to this cathedral of writing I have built. At my desk, my breathing slows down. I dissolve into the writing.

> This is the true joy in life, being used for a purpose recognized by yourself as a mighty one.
>
> —GEORGE BERNARD SHAW

I do not believe in fairy tales, and I don't think it's helpful to encourage others to believe in them either. As a species, we are self-destructing, and we are taking the rest of the world with us. I do believe in grace. If we open ourselves to the despair and pain of the world, and if, brokenhearted, we can still love the world, then we can become part of the medicine for the world.

Change writers who are not connected to the world generally cannot connect to readers. The pressures of the real world slow us down and beat us up. Pressures steal our time and fog our focus. Yet, in the end, these same pressures allow us to retain our membership in the human race.

Good storytellers heal the world. The stories that save us are the stories that give us what some Buddhists call a "bigger container." They open us up to new understanding and growth. Bigger container stories expand our circle of caring, and "complexify" the universe rather than simplify it. They encourage us to risk more for the world's sake rather than making us cynical, jaded, and cautious about it.

As writers, we can extend the circle of caring to plants and animals, to rivers and oceans and coral reefs. And we can form a caring circle of human beings that includes young and old, rich and poor, gay and straight, the immigrant, the homeless, the emotionally sturdy and the mentally ill, and those in prison, no matter what their religion. I would even include "terrorists" in the circle. They too are human, and can only be properly dealt with if we see them as people with needs, desires, and ideals like ourselves. Ultimately, placing them outside the circle only will hurt all of us. When any humans are dehumanized, we all lose some of our humanity. We are all mirrors looking into mirrors.

When I researched *The Middle of Everywhere,* I met Dep, a thin, dark-skinned Vietnamese girl who wore her hair in braids and dressed in the same gray sweat suit all year round. She lived with an impoverished, ill grandmother, and no doubt was clinically depressed. For nine months, Dep's teacher and I tried to coax her to speaking, but she remained silent. Then, the last week of school, we watched a film about lotus flowers in Southeast Asia. The lotus is a symbol of resiliency because it blooms pure white in mud. The film was narrated by a young Vietnamese girl, and, at the end of the film, Dep whispered to me, "That girl looks like me."

Our writing is one way in which we express our moral sense and our integrity. Morality is not a delicate consommé; it is a thick and spicy *jambong,* a concoction of fish, shrimp, squid, chilies, vegetables, and noodles, served in a flavorful dark broth. It is pungent, intriguing, and sustaining.

Morality involves specific acts at specific times and in specific places. It is the father who sits up all night by his ill baby daughter's crib, the wife who cares for her husband who can no longer speak, the girl who shares her lunch with another student poorer than herself, or the doctor who keeps operating and suturing as bombs fall around her. It is the graduate student who writes a play about eating disorders, or the scientist who explains the implications of his work, or the theologian who helps us grapple with the tragedy of the hour, or the musician who sings for peace.

The finest thing we can do in life is to grow a soul and then use it in the service of humankind. Writers foster the growth of readers' souls, and the best soil for growth is love. Writing can be love made visible. In the end, one of our best ways to truly change readers is to love them. We can create a world in which those who know teach those who wish to learn. We writers may not live to see the changes that we work for, but readers will enjoy the shade of the trees we have planted.

Czeslaw Milosz, the Polish poet and social activist, died on August 14, 2004, at the age of ninety-three. In remembrance, Leon Wieseltier wrote, "He had the rare gift of knowing how to be at once troubled and unperturbed. When light was needed he was light. When stone was needed he was stone."

Wieseltier tells us that while Milosz fought with the Polish Underground during World War II, he also produced a poetic masterpiece called "The World." He continues: "There are two ways of resisting evil: engagement and disengagement, attachment and detachment: action against it and contemplation despite it. In his dark era, Milosz was the master of this complication, this salvation, of consciousness."

The life of Czeslaw Milosz offers us a model for steadiness. He lived through a harsh time with creativity and courage. That is our challenge: To cultivate lives of reflection, love, and joy and still somehow manage to do our share for this beautiful broken planet of ours.

Margaret Mead defined an ideal culture as one that makes a place for every human gift. As our world approaches the precipice of destruction, it will survive only if we construct a new culture that is, to quote F. Scott Fitzgerald, "Something commensurate with our capacity for wonder." With our healing stories, we will build that good, strong place where every being is valued and every gift can shine forth.

Recommended Readings

MEMOIR AND BIOGRAPHY

Ruth Behar. *Translated Woman: Crossing the Border with Esperanza's Story*. Beacon Press, 2003.

Vera Brittain. *Testament of Youth*. Penguin, 2005.

Fox Butterworth. *All God's Children*. HarperCollins, 1996.

Forrest Carter. *The Education of Little Tree*. University of New Mexico Press, 2001.

Robert Caro. *The Path to Power: The Years of Lyndon Johnson*. Vol. 1. Knopf, 1982.

George Washington Carver. *George Washington Carver: In His Own Words*. University of Missouri Press, 1996.

Pablo Casals. *Joys and Sorrows*. Touchstone, 1970.

Da Chen. *Colors of the Mountain*. Anchor Press, 2001.

Cathy Davidson. *Thirty-six Views of Mt. Fuji: On Finding Myself in Japan*. Plume, 1994.

Drs. Sampson Davis, George Jenkins, and Rameck Hunt. *The Pact: Three Young Men Make a Promise and Fulfill a Dream*. Riverhead, 2003.

Annie Dillard. *Pilgrim at Tinker Creek*. HarperCollins, 1998.

Barbara Ehrenreich. *Nickle and Dimed: On (Not) Getting By in America*. Holt, 2002.

Ben Franklin. *The Autobiography of Benjamin Franklin*. Simon and Schuster, 2004.

Anne Garrels. *Naked in Baghdad: The Iraq War and Aftermath as Seen by NPR's Correspondent*. Picador, 2004.

Eugenia Ginzburg. *Into the Whirlwind*. Harcourt, 2003.

———. *Within the Whirlwind*. Northwestern University Press, 1997.

Jennifer Gonnerman. *Life on the Outside: The Prison Odyssey of Elaine Bartlett*. Picador, 2005.

Temple Grandin. *Thinking in Pictures: And Other Reports from My Life with Autism*. Random House, 1996.

John Howard Griffin. *Black Like Me*. Signet, 1997.

Paul Gruchow. *Grassroots: The Universe of Home*. Milkweed, 1995.

Doris Grumbach. *Coming Into the End Zone.* Norton, 1991.

John Gunther. *Death Be Not Proud.* HarperCollins, 1998.

Bill Holm. *The Music of Failure.* Milkweed, 2000.

Helen Keller. *Helen Keller: The Story of My Life.* Signet, 2002.

Tracy Kidder. *Mountains Beyond Mountains: The Quest of Dr. Paul Farmer, a Man who Would Cure the World.* Random House, 2003.

Joe Klein. *Woody Guthrie: A Life.* Dell, 1999.

Ted Kooser. *Local Wonders: Seasons in the Bohemian Alps.* University of Nebraska Press, 2004.

Aung San Suu Kyi. *Freedom from Fear.* Penguin, 1996.

Primo Levi. *Survival in Auschwitz.* Simon and Schuster, 1996.

Beverly Lowry. *Crossed Over: A Murder, a Memoir.* Random House, 2002.

Nelson Mandela. *A Long Walk to Freedom: The Autobiography of Nelson Mandela.* Little, Brown, 1995.

Mark Mathabane. *Kaffir Boy.* Simon and Schuster, 1998.

James McBride. *The Color of Water: A Black Man's Tribute to His White Mother.* Riverhead, 1997.

Namu Merthieu and Christine Merthieu. *Leaving Mother Lake: A Girlhood at the Edge of the World.* Back Bay Books, 2004.

J. G. Myer. *Executive Blues: Down and Out in Corporate America.* Dell, 1996.

John Neihardt. *Black Elk Speaks: Being the Life Story of a Holy Man of the Oglala Sioux.* University of Nebraska Press, 2004.

Kathleen Norris. *The Cloister Walk.* Riverhead, 1997.

Zainab Salbi. *Between Two Worlds—Escape From Tyranny: Growing Up in the Shadow of Saddam.* Gotham Books, 2005.

Albert Schweitzer. *Out of My Life and Thought.* Johns Hopkins University Press, 1998.

Ernest Shackleton. *South: The Endurance Expedition.* Signet, 1999.

Joshua Wolfe Shank. *Lincoln's Melancholia: How Depression Challenged a President and Fueled His Greatness.* Houghton Mifflin, 2005.

Floyd Skloot. *In the Shadow of Memory.* Bison Books, 2004.

Joe Starita. *The Dull Knives of Pine Ridge: A Lakota Odyssey.* University of Nebraska Press, 2002.

Mark Twain. *The Autobiography of Mark Twain.* HarperCollins, 2000.

Booker T. Washington. *Up From Slavery.* Penguin, 1986.

Eudora Welty. *One Writer's Beginnings.* Harvard University Press, 1995.

Loung Ung. *First They Killed My Father: A Daughter of Cambodia Remembers.* HarperCollins, 2001.

Marie Vassiltchikov. *Berlin Diaries.* Vintage, 1998.

PSYCHOLOGY

Mihaly Csikszentmihalyi. *Flow: The Psychology of Optimal Experience.* HarperCollins, 1991.

William Doherty. *Soul Searching: Why Psychotherapy Must Promote Social Responsibility.* Basic Books, 1995.

Carol Gilligan. *In a Different Voice: Psychological Theory and Women's Development.* Harvard University Press, 1983.

Daniel Goleman. *Emotional Intelligence.* Bantam, 1997.

Kay Redfield Jamison. *Touched by Fire: Manic Depressive Illness and the Artistic Temperament.* Simon and Schuster, 1996.

Carl Jung. *Man and His Symbols.* Laurel Press, 1970.

Jean Kilbourne. *Can't Buy My Love: How Advertising Changes the Way We Think and Feel.* Simon and Schuster, 2000.

Margaret Mead. *Coming of Age in Samoa: A Psychological Study of Primitive Youth for Western Civilization.* HarperCollins, 2001.

David Myers and Letha Scanzoni. *The American Paradox: Spiritual Hunger in the Age of Plenty.* Yale University Press, 2000.

Neil Postman. *The Disappearance of Childhood.* Knopf, 1994.

Fred Rogers. *Mister Rogers Parenting Book: Helping to Understand Your Young Child.* Running Press, 2002.

Shinichi Suzuki. *Nurtured by Love.* Warner Books, 1986.

Julie Schor. *Born to Buy: The Commercialized Child in the Consumer Culture.* Simon and Schuster, 2004.

Edwin Schur. *The Americanization of Sex.* Temple University Press, 1989.

PHILOSOPHY AND SPIRITUALITY

Tara Brach. *Radical Acceptance: Embracing Your Life with the Heart of a Buddha.* Bantam, 2004.

Martin Buber. *I and Thou.* Simon and Schuster, 1976.

George Crane. *The Bones of the Master: A Journey to Secret Mongolia.* Bantam, 2001.

Pema Chödrön. *When Things Fall Apart: Heart Advice for Difficult Times.* Shambala, 2000.

His Holiness the Dalai Lama. *The Art of Happiness: A Handbook for Living.* Riverhead, 1998.

Baba Ram Dass. *Be Here Now.* Crown, 1976.

Viktor Frankl. *Man's Search for Meaning: An Introduction to Logotherapy.* Simon and Schuster, 1984.

Philip Gulley and James Mulholland. *If Grace Is True—Why God Will Save Every Person.* HarperCollins, 2004.

Thich Nhat Hanh. *Being Peace.* Parallax Press, 1988.

Charles Johnson. *Turning the Wheel: Essays on Buddhism and Writing.* Simon and Schuster, 2003.

Jack Kornfield. *A Path with a Heart—A Guide through the Perils and Promises of Everyday Life.* Bantam, 1993.

Anne Lamott. *Traveling Mercies: Thoughts on Faith.* Anchor Books, 2000.

Joanna Macy. *Coming Back to Life: Practices to Reconnect Our Lives, Our World.* New Society Publishing, 1998.

Stephen Mitchell, translator. *Tao Te Ching.* HarperCollins, 1992.

Wes Nisker. *Buddha's Nature—A Practical Guide to Discovering Your Place in the Cosmos.* Bantam, 2000.

Bertrand Russell. *Why I Am Not a Christian and Other Essays on Religion and Related Subjects.* Simon and Schuster, 1976.

Eckhart Tolle. *The Power of Now: A Guide for Spiritual Enlightenment.* New World Library, 1999.

Alice Walker. *Living by the Word.* Harcourt, 1988.

HISTORY

Daniel Bergner. *In the Land of Magic Soldiers: A Story of White and Black in West Africa.* Farrar, Straus and Giroux, 2003.

H. G. Bissinger. *Friday Night Lights.* DeCapo, 2003.

Iris Chang. *The Rape of Nanking: The Forgotten Holocaust of World War Two.* Penguin, 1998.

Winston Churchill. *The Gathering Storm.* Houghton Mifflin, 1948.

Stephanie Coontz. *Marriage—A History: From Obedience to Intimacy or How Love Conquered Marriage.* Viking, 2005.

Jared Diamond. *Collapse: How Societies Choose to Fail or Succeed.* Viking, 2004.

Melissa Fay Greene. *Praying for Sheetrock.* Random House, 1992.

Philip Gourevitch. *We Wish to Inform You That Tomorrow We Will Be Killed with Our Families: Stories from Rwanda.* Picador, 1999.

Adam Hochschild. *King Leopold's Ghosts: A Story of Greed, Terror and Heroism in Colonial Africa.* Houghton Mifflin, 1999.

Erik Larson and Isaac Monroe Cline. *Isaac's Storm: A Man, a Time and the Deadliest Hurricane in History.* Knopf, 2000.

Norman Maclean. *Young Men and Fire.* University of Chicago Press, 1993.

Elizabeth Neuffer. *The Key to My Neighbor's House: Seeking Justice in Bosnia and Rwanda.* Picador, 2002.

Eleanor Roosevelt. *My Day: The Best of Eleanor Roosevelt's Acclaimed Newspaper Columns 1936–1962.* MJF Books, 2005.

Pascal Khoo Thwe. *From the Land of Green Ghosts: A Burmese Odyssey.* HarperCollins, 2003.

Barbara Tuchman. *A Distant Mirror: The Calamitous Fourteenth Century.* Random House, 1979.

Howard Zinn. *A People's History of the United States.* HarperPerennial, 1995.

WRITING

Peter Elbow. *Writing with Power: Techniques to Mastering the Writing Process.* Oxford University Press, 1998.

Bonnie Friedman. *Writing Past Dark: Envy, Fear, Distractions, and Other Dilemmas in the Writer's Life.* HarperCollins, 1994.

John Gardner. *On Moral Fiction.* Basic Books, 1979.

Natalie Goldberg. *Writing Down the Bones: Freeing the Writer Within.* Shambhala, 2006.

Jane Hirshfield. *Nine Gates: Entering the Mind of Poetry.* HarperCollins, 1997.

Joseph Wood Krutch. *Five Masters: A Study in the Mutations of the Novel.* Smith Peter, 1990.

Anne Lamott. *Bird by Bird.* Knopf, 1995.

Bill Moyers. *Fooling With Words: A Celebration of Poets and Their Craft.* HarperCollins, 2000.

NONFICTION

Edward Abbey. *Desert Solitaire: A Season in Wilderness.* Random House, 1973.

Julia Alvarez. *A Cafecito Story.* Chelsea Green, 1989.

Alan AtKisson. *Believing Cassandra: An Optimist Looks at a Pessimist's World.* Chelsea Green, 1999.

James Baldwin. *The Fire Next Time.* Knopf, 1993.

Benjamin Barber. *Jihad vs. McWorld.* Ballantine, 1996.

Simone de Beauvoir. *The Second Sex.* Random House, 1990.

Wendell Berry. *What Are People For?* Farrar, Straus and Giroux, 1990.

Stephen Bloom. *Postville: A Clash of Cultures in Heartland America.* Harvest Books, 2001.

Carol Bly. *Changing the Bully Who Rules the World: Reading and Thinking About Ethics.* Milkweed, 1996.

Ira Byock. *Dying Well: Peace and Possibilities at the End of Life.* Riverhead, 1998.

Rachel Carson. *Silent Spring.* Houghton Mifflin, 2002.

Noam Chomsky. *Hegemony or Survival: America's Quest for Global Dominance.* Holt, 2004.

Robert Coles. *The Call of Service.* Houghton Mifflin, 1994.

Joe Dominguez and Vicki Robin. *Your Money or Your Life: Transforming Your Relationship with Money and Achieving Financial Independence.* Penguin, 2000.

Richard Dyer. *White.* Taylor and Francis, 1997.

Loren Eiseley. *The Immense Journey.* Knopf, 1976.

Duane Elgin. *Voluntary Simplicity: Toward a Way of Life That Is Outwardly Simple, Inwardly Rich.* HarperCollins, 1993.

Anne Fadiman. *The Spirit Catches You and You Fall Down: A Hmong Child, Her American Doctors, and the Collision of Two Cultures.* Farrar, Straus and Giroux, 1998.

William Finnegan. *Cold New World: Growing Up in a Harder Country.* Random House, 1999.

Thomas Friedman. *The Lexus and the Olive Tree: Understanding Globalization.* Knopf, 2000.

Buckminster Fuller. *Critical Path.* St. Martin's Press, 1982.

Susan Griffin. *Pornography and Silence: Culture's Revolt Against Nature.* HarperCollins, 1982.

Sarah Hardy. *Mother Nature: Maternal Instincts and How They Shape the Human Species.* Random House, 2005.

Václav Havel. *Open Letters: Selected Writing 1965–1990.* Knopf, 1992.

Adam Hochschild. *Mirror at Midnight: A South African Journey.* Viking, 1990.

Paula Huntley. *The Hemingway Book Club of Kosovo.* Tarcher, 2004.

Pico Iyer. *The Global Soul: Jet Lag, Shopping Malls, and the Search for Home.* Knopf, 2001.

LeAlan Jones and Lloyd Newman, with David Isay. *Our America: Life and Death on the South Side of Chicago.* Simon and Schuster, 1998 .

Jawanza Kunjufu. *Countering the Conspiracy to Destroy Black Boys.* African American Images, 1987.

George Lakoff. *Don't Think of an Elephant: Know Your Values and Frame the Debate: The Essential Guide for Progressives.* Chelsea Green, 2004.

Aldo Leopold. *Sand County Almanac: With Essays on Conservation from Round River.* Random House, 1970.

Paul Rogat Loeb. *Soul of a Citizen: Living with Conviction in a Cynical Time.* St. Martin's Press, 1999.

Bill McKibben. *The Age of Missing Information.* Plume, 1993.

Donella Meadows, Dennis Meadows, and Jorgan Randers. *Limits to Growth: The Thirty-Year Update*. Chelsea Green, 2004.

Czeslaw Milosz. *Legends of Modernity: Essays and Letters from Occupied Poland*. Farrar, Straus and Giroux, 2005.

Katherine Newman, David Harding, and Cybele Fox. *Rampage: The Social Roots of the School Shootings*. Basic Books, 2005.

Thomas Paine. *Common Sense*. Bantam, 2003.

Parker Palmer. *The Courage to Teach: Exploring the Inner Landscape of a Teacher's Life*. Jossey-Bass, 1997.

Samantha Power. *A Problem from Hell: America and the Age of Genocide*. HarperCollins, 2003.

Erik Reece. *Lost Mountain*. Riverhead, 2006.

Howard Rheingold. *Smart Mobs: The Next Social Revolution*. Basic Books, 2003.

Adrienne Rich. *Of Woman Born—Motherhood as Experience and Institution*. Norton, 1986.

Arundhati Roy. *Power Politics*. South End Press, 2002.

Carl Sagan. *Cosmos*. Random House, 1985.

Mark Salzman. *True Notebooks: A Writer's Year at Juvenile Hall*. Knopf, 2004.

Scott Russell Sanders. *Staying Put: Making a Home in a Restless World*. Beacon Press, 1994.

Eric Schlosser. *Fast Food Nation: The Dark Side of the All-American Meal*. Harper-Collins, 2002.

Susan Sontag. *Illness as Metaphor and AIDS and Its Metaphors*. St. Martin's Press, 2001.

Betsy Taylor. *What Kids Really Want That Money Can't Buy*. Warner Books, 2003.

Terry Tempest Williams. *Refuge: An Unnatural History of Family and Place*. Knopf, 1992.

Studs Terkel. *Working: People Talk About What They Do All Day and How They Feel About What They Do*. New Press, 1997.

Lewis Thomas. *The Lives of a Cell*. Penguin, 1975.

Henry David Thoreau. *Walden and On Civil Disobedience*. Barnes and Noble, 2005.

Cornel West. *Democracy Matters: Winning the Fight Against Imperialism*. Penguin Press, 2005.

Frank Wu. *Yellow: Race in America Beyond Black and White*. Basic Books, 2003.

FICTION

Chinua Achebe. *Things Fall Apart*. Doubleday, 1994.

Chimamanda Nqozi Adichie. *Purple Hibiscus*. Knopf, 2004.

Sherman Alexie. *The Lone Ranger and Tonto Fistfight in Heaven*. Grove/Atlantic, 2005.

Julia Alvarez. *In the Time of the Butterflies.* Plume, 1995.

Ray Bradbury. *Farenheit 451.* Random House, 1972.

Andre Brink. *A Dry White Season.* Penguin, 1984.

Pearl S. Buck. *The Good Earth.* Simon and Schuster, 2004.

Albert Camus. *The Plague.* Knopf, 1991.

Raymond Carver. *Cathedral.* Knopf, 1989.

Willa Cather. *My Ántonia.* Houghton Mifflin, 1995.

Miguel de Cervantes. *Don Quixote.* Signet, 2001.

Charles Dickens. *Pickwick Papers.* Oxford University Press, 1998.

Isak Dinesen. *Out of Africa.* Random House, 1992.

Fyodor Dostoevsky. *The Brothers Karamazov.* Barnes and Noble, 2004.

Andre Dubus III. *House of Sand and Fog.* Knopf, 2000.

Ralph Ellison *The Invisible Man.* Knopf, 1995.

Leif Enger. *Peace Like a River.* Grove/Atlantic, 2002.

Nikolay Gogol. *The Overcoat.* Dover, 1992.

William Golding. *Lord of the Flies.* Perigee, 1959.

Nadine Gordimer. *July's People.* Penguin, 1982.

Günter Grass. *The Tin Drum.* Knopf, 1989.

Kent Haruf. *Plainsong.* Knopf, 2000.

Ursula Hegi. *Stones from the River.* Simon and Schuster, 1997.

Ernest Hemingway. *For Whom the Bell Tolls.* Simon and Schuster, 1995.

John Hershey. *Hiroshima.* Knopf, 1989.

Victor Hugo. *Les Miserables.* Barnes and Noble, 2003.

Henry James. *The Turn of the Screw.* TOR Books, 1993.

Ha Jin. *Waiting.* Knopf, 2000.

Charles Johnson. *Middle Passage.* Simon and Schuster, 1998.

Franz Kafka. *The Transformation: Metamorphosis and Other Stories.* Penguin, 1995.

Stephanie Kallos. *Broken for You.* Grove/Atlantic, 2005.

Barbara Kingsolver. *The Poisonwood Bible.* HarperCollins, 2003.

Milan Kundera. *The Book of Laughter and Forgetting.* HarperCollins, 1999.

Jhumpa Lahiri. *The Namesake.* Houghton Mifflin, 2004.

Halldor Laxness. *Independent People.* Random House, 1996.

Chang-rae Lee. *A Gesture Life.* Riverhead, 2000.

Harper Lee. *To Kill a Mockingbird.* HarperCollins, 2002.

Doris Lessing. *The Golden Notebooks.* HarperCollins, 1999.

Thomas Mann. *The Magic Mountain.* Knopf, 1996.

Yann Martel. *Life of Pi.* Harcourt, 2003.

Armistead Maupin. *Maybe the Moon.* HarperCollins, 1993.

Anchee Min. *Becoming Madame Mao.* Houghton Mifflin, 2001.

Rohinton Mistry. *A Fine Balance.* Random House, 2001.

Tim O'Brien. *The Things They Carried.* Random House, 1998.

Michael Ondaatje. *Anil's Ghost.* Knopf, 2001.

George Orwell. *Animal Farm.* Signet, 1996.

————. *1984.* Signet, 1976.

Ruth Ozeki. *My Year of Meats.* Penguin, 1995.

Cynthia Ozick. *Heir to the Glimmering World.* Houghton Mifflin, 2005.

Ann Pachett. *Bel Canto.* HarperCollins, 2001.

Boris Pasternak. *Doctor Zhivago.* Knopf, 1991.

Alan Paton. *Cry, the Beloved Country.* Simon and Schuster, 2003.

Chaim Potok. *The Chosen.* Random House, 1976.

Marcel Proust. *Remembrance of Things Past.* Random House, 1981.

Daniel Quinn. *Ishmael.* Bantam, 1995.

Erich Maria Remarque. *All Quiet on the Western Front.* Random House, 1976.

Marilynne Robinson. *Gilead.* Farrar, Straus and Giroux, 2004.

Arundhati Roy. *The God of Small Things.* HarperCollins 1998.

Mark Salzman. *The Soloist.* Knopf, 1995.

José Saramago. *Blindness.* Harcourt, 1999.

Asne Seierstad. *The Bookseller of Kabul.* Little, Brown, 2004.

Upton Sinclair. *The Jungle.* Dover, 2001.

Isaac Bashevis Singer. "Androgynous," in *Collected Stories of Isaac Bashevis Singer.* Farrar, Straus and Giroux, 1982.

Zadie Smith. *White Teeth.* Knopf, 2001.

Wallace Stegner. *Joe Hill: A Biographical Novel.* Penguin, 1990.

John Steinbeck. *The Grapes of Wrath.* Penguin, 2002.

Harriet Beecher Stowe. *Uncle Tom's Cabin.* Bantam, 1981.

William Styron. *Confessions of Nat Turner.* Knopf, 1993.

Leo Tolstoy. *War and Peace.* Signet, 1976.

Mark Twain. *The Adventures of Huckleberry Finn.* Barnes and Noble, 2004.

James Welch. *Winter in the Blood.* Penguin, 1986.

POETRY AND PLAYS

Anna Akhmatova. *Poems of Akhmatova: Izbrannye Stikhi.* Houghton Mifflin, 1997.

Rob Brezsny. *Pronoia is the Antidote for Paranoia: How the Whole World Is Conspiring to Shower You with Blessings.* Frog LTD, 2005.

Carolyn Forche. *The Angel of History.* HarperCollins, 1995.

Robert Frost. *Robert Frost's Poems.* St. Martin's Press, 2002.

Allen Ginsberg. *Collected Poems, 1947–1980.* Harper and Row, 1988.

Joy Harjo. *She Had Some Horses.* Thunder Mountain Press, 1997.

Robert Hass, editor. *The Essential Haiku: Versions of Basho, Buson and Issa.* Vol. 20. HarperCollins, 1994.

Federico García Lorca. *The House of Bernada Alba: A Drama About Women in Villages in Spain.* Dramatists Play Service, 1999.

Arthur Miller. *All My Sons.* Dramatists Play Service, 1951.

Pablo Neruda. *Twenty Love Poems and A Song of Despair.* Penguin, 2003.

Mary Oliver. *New and Selected Poems.* Vol. 1. Beacon, 2004.

Eugene O'Neill. *The Iceman Cometh.* Knopf, 2000.

William Stafford. *Even in Quiet Places.* Confluence Press, 1996.

Walt Whitman. *Leaves of Grass.* Signet, 2000.

CHILDREN'S BOOKS

Louisa May Alcott. *Little Women.* Signet, 2004.

Marion Dane Bauer. *What's Your Story: A Young Person's Guide to Writing Fiction.* Houghton Mifflin, 1992.

Pearl S. Buck. *The Big Wave.* HarperCollins, 1973.

Frances Hodgson Burnett. *A Little Princess.* HarperCollins, 1991.

Barry Denenberg. *The Journal of Ben Uchida, Citizen # 13559.* Scholastic, 2003.

Anne Frank. *The Diary of Anne Frank.* Bantam, 1997.

Antoine de Saint-Exupéry. *The Little Prince.* Harcourt, 2000.

Ian Serraillier. *Escape from Warsaw (The Silver Sword).* Scholastic, 1990.

Anna Sewell. *Black Beauty.* Dover, 1999.

Shel Silverstein. *A Light in the Attic.* HarperCollins, 1981.

Betty Smith. *A Tree Grows in Brooklyn.* HarperCollins, 2005.

E. B. White. *Charlotte's Web.* HarperCollins, 1952.

Acknowledgments

Thanks to Jim, Sara, Zeke and Jamie, Kate, Aidan and Claire, who kept my heart happy, Toni and Jane Bray, John and Joy Bray, Karleen Bright, Steve and Pam Beyers, Max and Henrietta Isbell, Paul Isbell, Roberta and Allen Harrison, Bernard Pipher, and Pam and Lee Wilhelm and all my other family members.

And thanks to Pam Barger, Beatty Brasch, Joette Byrd, Twyla Hanson, Lynda Madison, Jill and Reynold Peterson, Marge Saiser, Barb Schmitz, Carl Schreiner, Karen Shoemaker, Janice Spellerberg, and Jan Stenberg.

And thank you to those who helped with this book—Deb Hauswald, Don Helmuth, Mohamed Jalloh, Marian Langan, Kelly Madigan-Erlandson, Beth Myers, David G. Myers, DiAnna Schimek, Rich Simon, Chris Sommerich, Ray Stevens, Terry Werner, Steve Woofter, and Jan Zegers.

Thanks to my first teachers—Bill Kloefkorn, Kent Haruf, Leon Satterfield, Charles Stubblefield—and my first editor and dear friend, Jane Isay, to JoAnn Miller at Basic Books, and to my loyal agent, Susan Lee Cohen, and to my friend and advocate at Riverhead, Susan Petersen Kennedy, to Celina Spiegel, who helped me create this book, to Charlotte Douglas, and to my new editor, Jake Morrissey, and my fine publicist, Mih-ho Cha, who worked so diligently on my behalf, I appreciate all of you dear ones.

ABOUT THE AUTHOR

Mary Pipher, Ph.D., is the author of seven books, including the *New York Times* bestsellers *Reviving Ophelia*, *The Shelter of Each Other*, and *Another Country*. Her work has been translated into more than twenty-five languages, and she has lectured to groups and conferences around the world. Dr. Pipher is interested in how American culture affects the mental health of its people; her writing has been influenced by her rural background, her training in both psychology and anthropology, and her years as a therapist. She lives in Lincoln, Nebraska, with her husband, Jim, near their children and grandchildren.